SEGMENTATION
MARKETING

SEGMENTATION MARKETING

New Methods for Capturing Business Markets

JOHN BERRIGAN and CARL FINKBEINER

NATIONAL ANALYSTS, INC.

With contributions by Shel Feldman

HarperBusiness
A Division of HarperCollins*Publishers*

HarperCollins books may be purchased for educational, business, or sales promotional use. For information, please write: Special Markets Department, HarperCollins Publishers, Inc., 10 East 53rd Street, New York, NY 10022.

FIRST EDITION

Designed by Irving Perkins Associates

Library of Congress Cataloging-in-Publication Data

Berrigan, John.
Segmentation marketing : new methods for capturing business markets / John Berrigan, Carl Finkbeiner, with contributions by Shel Feldman.
p. cm.
Includes bibliographical references and index.
ISBN 0-88730-558-X
1. Market segmentation. I. Finkbeiner, Carl. II. Title.
HF5415.127.B47 1992
658.8'02—dc20 91-58501

---

93 94 95 96 PS/RRD 10 9 8 7 6 5 4 3 2

To our families:
Dorothy, Kristen, Daniel, David
Dru, Elise, Carly
For your extraordinary support and patience,
our love and gratitude.

CONTENTS

Contents

Contents

Contents

PREFACE

When the dust settles from internally focused efforts such as employee motivation, restructuring, and cost-cutting, management is forced to turn its attention to the fundamental battleground—the market. Faced with increasing competition on a global scale, the market challenge is to produce a continuous competitive advantage at acceptable margins. The winners in this highly competitive environment will develop processes that efficiently create and deliver products and services that respond to customer needs in a timely manner.

Based on 10 years of research and consulting experience, this book describes a proven, practical, cost-effective approach for creating a sustained differential advantage in business markets. The cornerstone of the approach is needs-based segmentation marketing—a technique used successfully in consumer marketing, but not adequately transferred to business markets.

Needs-based segmentation marketing begins with the identification of needs that customers attempt to satisfy when buying products and services. A cost-effective competitive advantage is created by segmenting customers into groups with similar patterns of need and then targeting product development, marketing, and sales efforts toward the satisfaction of the needs of segments that offer the greatest revenue and profitability potential. Monitoring and responding to segment needs sustains that competitive advantage.

Until now the presence of multiple decision makers, and therefore multiple sources of need, has been a handicap to those who sought to transfer successful needs-based segmentation techniques from consumer to business market applications. This book presents a proven technique for identifying and segmenting the needs of multiple purchase influencers among business buyers. However, the technique is only the starting point for effective segmentation marketing. The true competitive power of segmentation marketing is realized by translating the segmentation into integrated strategic and tactical actions. To help you fully leverage segmentation, we provide step-by-step guidelines for implementing and applying segmentation marketing. Because successful segmentation marketing requires a holistic, integrated approach to the market involving strategic planning, marketing, product development, sales, and many other functional activities, this book cuts across many disciplines.

Those who develop strategies designed to create and sustain a differential competitive advantage should read this book because theirs is the responsibility for creating the discipline and motivation that will produce a holistic, integrated approach to the market. Market, product, and sales management will benefit from learning how to use segmentation tools to create a sustained advantage. Market researchers will learn how to build the information and analytic tools necessary to support segmentation marketing. Future business leaders who are in school will gain insight into the complex process of marketing and selling products and services to businesses. Scholars working in the field of business marketing are invited to search the approach for areas that warrant further investigation. We hope the contents of this book will stimulate all of these audiences to action.

John Berrigan
Carl Finkbeiner
February 1992

ACKNOWLEDGMENTS

We bear a special debt of gratitude to Shel Feldman of the Wisconsin Center for Demand-Side Research. Shel is a good friend and colleague who participated in many of our early discussions and helped shape our initial thinking on business segmentation. He even went so far as to write a draft of Chapter 6, "Tactical Applications of Needs-Based Segmentation." For all of his contributions, we give Shel our heartfelt thanks.

Many organizations and individuals have contributed to the ideas presented in this book. The Electric Power Research Institute and its electric utility membership deserve significant credit for supporting the Customer Preference and Behavior Project (2671) that produced the research and pilot testing of the segmentation methodology and tools presented in this book. We would especially like to thank Clark Gellings, Larry Lewis, and Thom Henneberger for their insights and enthusiastic support. Member utilities who deserve recognition for their willingness to pilot these techniques include Wisconsin Electric Company, Baltimore Gas & Electric, Duke Power, and the Snohomish County P.U.D.

Several other client organizations and staff made significant contributions to the evolution of the framework and methods described in the book. Our thanks to Pacific Bell and Melinda Denton for supporting the early efforts in business segmentation from which the segmentation framework described in this book evolved. Also, we would like to extend our gratitude to the Strategic Marketing staff at US West including Ron Rinkle and Greg Gum for the opportunity to demonstrate how qualitative research can be used to reveal business customer needs.

A special thanks is extended to the IBM Corporation and the staff within Network Systems and Enterprise Systems for the insights and support that enabled us to apply the segmentation framework described here to the complex world of information systems and communications. Of particular note are the contributions of Maurie Prauner, Denis O'Shea, Ed Michels, Brenda Isaacs, Barbara Dobbins, Cathy Bahan, and Janet Streicher on the Network Systems project. Members of the Enterprise Systems project who contributed to our thinking include Ed Robbins, Gwen Scalpello, Ron Dombroski, John Young, and Pat Van Waes.

This book would not have been possible without the support of Booz • Allen & Hamilton and the creative contributions of colleagues and friends who have worked with us during the last few years. At the risk of offending those who are forgotten, we begin by thanking Bill Michels, vice president and head of the Computer Information Systems Group. As a reader of the initial draft, Bill provided extraordinary insight that permitted us to reshape this book to fit the needs of the practitioner. Beyond his editorial support, Bill's enthusiastic endorsement of the approach has been a continuous source of inspiration. Also, we owe a debt of gratitude to Karen Abarbenal who applied her editorial skills to translate technical jargon into readable English. Other friends and colleagues at Booz • Allen who shaped our thinking include Tom Williams, Steve Grody, and Andre Jezierski.

We would like to extend our gratitude to Steve Nowick, president of the VSAT Division of Scientific Atlanta, for his thoughtful contributions as a reader. Steve, like Bill Michels, spent considerable time and effort to carefully read and thoughtfully comment on the text. We know they will notice their contributions; we valued them greatly.

We have benefited enormously from the support of management, friends, and colleagues at National Analysts who have worked directly with us to apply the methods and tools described in this book as well as to create this text. Marshall Greenberg, former president of National Analysts, served as a mentor and editor. His early applications of needs-based segmentation in consumer markets provided the inspiration and intellectual direction that enabled us to make the translation of needs-based segmentation techniques to business markets. Al Hall supervised the background research noted in the bibliography. We are particularly grateful to Donna McAdams, Minerva Medina, and Margaret McLoughney, who not only supervised but actually prepared the manuscript for publication. Donna, Minerva, and Margaret received considerable assistance from Larry Bansbach in proofing and Debbie Argento in graphics at National Analysts.

A special thanks to Virginia Smith, our editor, as well as others at HarperCollins for their patience and support.

INTRODUCTION

SEGMENTATION MARKETING: KEY CONCEPTS

Every business seller is discovering that the ability to establish a profitable and sustainable market position is becoming extremely difficult. The number of competitors is increasing, and they come in all sizes and shapes from all parts of the globe. Competition comes from giants with deep pockets as well as modestly financed niche players who simply nibble market share. The competition is Japanese, European, South American, or "made in the U.S.A." And, to make matters worse, even the most insulated industries are expanding sales territories to global markets.

Once-secure competitive strategies such as cost leadership and product differentiation are failing. Even the most lean and mean low-cost position is temporary. Small, agile cutthroats as well as large government subsidized competitors can undercut virtually any low-cost strategy. Moreover, the ease and speed with which technology can be copied or even surpassed has significantly reduced the staying power of a strategy based solely on smaller, faster, or more innovative products.

In this evolving, highly competitive environment, the holy grail is a sustainable advantage. As the search intensifies, there is a bewildering array of "secret maps." Among these maps to success are downsizing, restructuring, quality improvement, customer satisfaction, value delivery, hands-on management, and employee empowerment. While each has merit, no one map has delivered an enduring competitive advantage to any of its users.

This book offers a different route to the grail specially designed for those who sell products and services to other businesses. The approach is constructed on a firm foundation of experience complemented by common sense. Unlike others, it is not dependent on a single focus such as quality or downsizing; instead, it advocates adoption of a comprehensive vision grounded in the fundamental "blocking and tackling" activities of marketing and selling. Although we are convinced our approach is correct, it is not a panacea. To make it work requires commitment, hard work, and time.

AN OVERVIEW OF THE APPROACH

The underlying premise of our approach is that timely, cost-effective products and services that satisfy customer needs will produce a sustainable competitive advantage. The challenge is to create a process that delivers such products and services.

The Vision

It is our view that business customers acquire products and services to satisfy needs. In the complex world of business decision making, there are multiple sources of needs reflecting domains of influence within the business infrastructure. As Exhibit 1 indicates, senior management possesses needs that are related to the shaping of the business's strategy. The needs of overall operations management are geared to policies and procedures designed to implement the strategy. At an even deeper level of management, function managers (like MIS directors) have needs that are closely tied to managing specific functional operations and to the products and services that must be acquired to keep the business running.

A sustainable competitive advantage is created by implementing a cost-effective, disciplined, and cross-functionally integrated process for identifying and monitoring these needs

Exhibit 1
DOMAINS OF INFLUENCE MAPPED TO CATEGORIES OF NEED

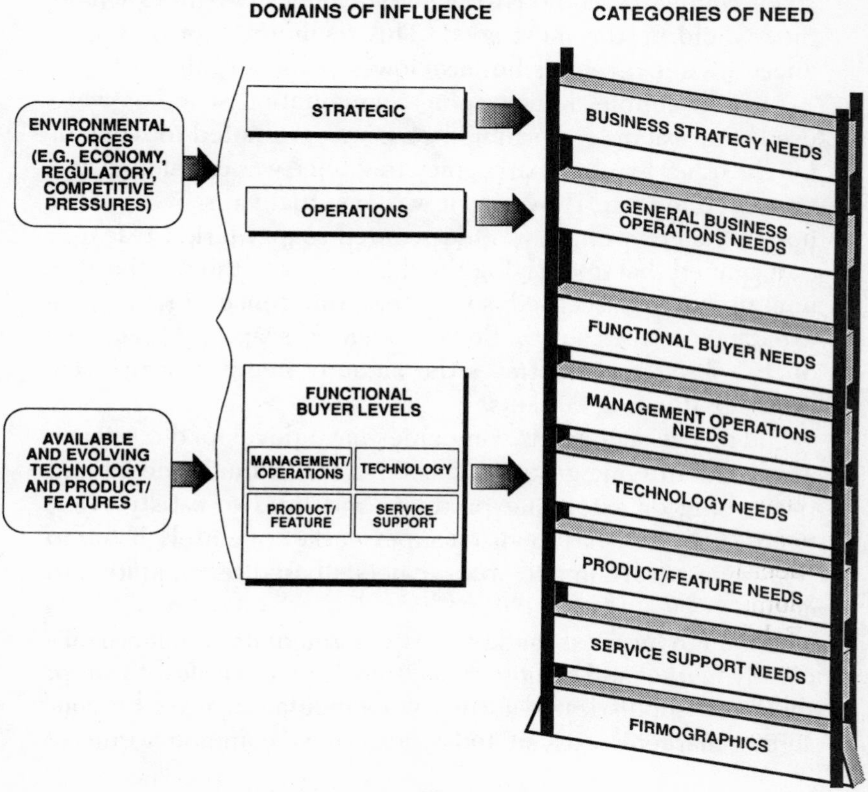

DOMAINS OF INFLUENCE

CATEGORIES OF NEED

ENVIRONMENTAL FORCES (E.G., ECONOMY, REGULATORY, COMPETITIVE PRESSURES)

STRATEGIC

OPERATIONS

AVAILABLE AND EVOLVING TECHNOLOGY AND PRODUCT/ FEATURES

FUNCTIONAL BUYER LEVELS

MANAGEMENT/ OPERATIONS | TECHNOLOGY

PRODUCT/ FEATURE | SERVICE SUPPORT

BUSINESS STRATEGY NEEDS

GENERAL BUSINESS OPERATIONS NEEDS

FUNCTIONAL BUYER NEEDS

MANAGEMENT OPERATIONS NEEDS

TECHNOLOGY NEEDS

PRODUCT/FEATURE NEEDS

SERVICE SUPPORT NEEDS

FIRMOGRAPHICS

and then developing, marketing, and selling products and services that satisfy these needs in a timely fashion. The cornerstone of this process is needs-based segmentation.

Needs-based Segmentation

The concept of segmentation has its roots in consumer marketing where package goods companies like Procter & Gamble recognized the value of Machiavelli's advice "divide and rule." By dividing consumers into groups or segments, package goods companies could cost effectively focus resources where they would do the most good. This technique not only produced higher revenues but also lower costs per sale.

At first, simple demographic segmentation schemes were used. For example, perfumed soap was promoted to women. On the other hand, a sharp, spicy fragrance was developed and promoted to men. However, it was eventually discovered that not all men or women wanted scented soap. Market research determined that underlying the differences in the purchase or nonpurchase of scented soap were differences in needs—avoidance of allergic reactions to scented soaps, for example. Such a discovery illustrates the value of needs as a primary means of dividing markets.

Today, package goods companies have developed a science around identifying groups of customers with similar needs and developing or extending products and lines to satisfy those needs. One only has to visit a supermarket or closely listen to television advertising to observe needs-based segmentation in action.

Although business marketers use segmentation to more efficiently market and sell products, they have been slow to adopt the more sophisticated forms of segmentation used by consumer marketers. Even today, the most common forms of business market segmentation are based on simple "firm-ographics" such as industry type, size, and usage. It is not unusual to find a segmentation that includes Kmart, Nordstroms, and Bloomingdale's in the same segment, despite the fact that these large retailers tend to acquire different products and services. For instance, consistent with its strategic need to remain price competitive, Kmart tends to acquire technologies that will reduce operations expenses while Nordstroms puts quality and customer comfort first when buying products and services.

In the face of the success of their colleagues in consumer marketing, why have business marketers ignored needs-based segmentation? There are two possible explanations. First, the complexity of business decision making intimidates business marketers, forcing them to seek shelter in simpler albeit more ineffective segmentation methods. Or second, business decision making is perceived as more rational than consumer purchasing behavior. This rational model assumes that all business purchase decisions are ultimately driven by economics, not by needs.

This book addresses both of these barriers to the use of needs-based segmentation. Applying a considerable body of research conducted in business markets for numerous clients spanning several industries and product and service categories, we have developed a segmentation framework that captures the complexity of business decision making in a simple, easy-to-use form. Moreover, as the Nordstroms example implies, the framework makes it clear that financial factors alone do not determine purchase decisions.

While the techniques of customer-needs research and segmentation create the platform, it is the application of the information blended with a systematic, disciplined, and integrated implementation process that actually produces the sustainable competitive advantage.

The Applications

Once research is completed and markets are segmented and sized, the most important activity begins—selecting target segments that offer the most opportunity in growth, profits, and potential differentiation relative to capabilities. These segment choices will guide subsequent strategic investment decisions in product development, manufacturing, marketing, sales, and distribution. Products, product packages, and product portfolios are developed in accordance with the needs of the target segments. In addition, pricing, competitive positioning, advertising messages, and service, as well as sales and distribution channels, are shaped to be responsive to target segment needs.

To get the most out of the segmentation, we provide detailed guidelines, lessons learned, and tools related to key applications such as market selection, product portfolio analysis, competitive positioning, product packaging, and sales. Furthermore, to help you stay ahead of the competition and deliver products and services that customers want when they want them, we include instructions and tools for periodic tracking of needs and segment membership. And, finally, we offer direction on performance monitoring to help you evaluate how well you are doing and to identify performance gaps.

Implementation

In practice, we have found that reliable, current information about customer needs, the most advanced segmentation framework, and analytic tools and sound guidelines on application techniques are wasted if they are not implemented in a systematic, disciplined, and integrated manner. Among the most critical barriers to implementation are attitudes toward change and perception of turf. These can be addressed through a conscious educational effort designed to create understanding about the uses and benefits of the approach. Nevertheless, the keys to acceptance are feelings of ownership among relevant functional areas complemented by perceptions that the approach will produce results that benefit the participants.

In our experience, understanding and acceptance contribute heavily to a willingness to invest in the discipline that is necessary if activities are to be coordinated across functional areas. Activity coordination—different functional groups working together, sharing information and analytics to achieve a common objective—is essential to effective response to customer needs. For instance, product development must work and share information with marketing. Similarly, marketing must share information and support sales and distribution. Such coordination is facilitated by acceptance of a common framework for understanding the market.

The Benefits of the Approach

In the struggle to grow revenues, maintain acceptable profits, and fend off competition in an increasingly competitive market, firms that sell products and services to business must develop a sustainable competitive advantage. This book offers a comprehensive method for producing a competitive advantage that can withstand the test of time and increasing competition. The competitive advantage is based on the creation of value for the customer through the development and promotion of products and services that are differentiated by meeting the customer's needs and by being available when the customer wants them.

The use of a needs-based segmentation framework that represents the complexity of the business decision-making process offers several additional benefits. First, segmentation promotes selective investments in markets that are likely to yield higher rates of return. Second, segmentation contributes to efficient marketing and selling by focusing efforts on groups of customers whose needs are compatible with your products and services. Third, marketing and selling efforts can produce higher hit rates at lower costs per sale because needs-based segmentation enables you to develop tailored marketing positions and selling messages that hit the buyers' hot buttons even when there are multiple buyers.

Product development can benefit from needs-based segmentation. First, the identification of met and unmet customer needs in the context of segments promotes a cost-effective focus on product development activities that will generate products that strategically valued customers want. Second, success rates of new products, product packages, and product extensions can be improved because the use of a segmentation framework allows product development to design products that account for the feature and packaging preferences of targeted segments. Finally, economies of scale can be created by designing groups or portfolios of products and services targeted to segments that are likely to offer higher returns on investment.

By using the needs-based segmentation tools described here for prospecting and selling, sales departments can realize considerable benefits. First, segmentation and the pre-qualification of customers into segments enables sales to be more selective and to increase hit rates. Second, armed with needs profiles for segments, sales can tailor the message to fit the customer, thereby increasing the likelihood of a sale. Third, the use of a needs framework that accounts for multiple decision makers and products permits the salesperson to shape the message to the needs of a particular influencer on the purchase, thereby increasing selling chances and reducing the likelihood of vetos by senior management. Finally, product portfolio strategies designed to fit the needs of different target segments allow the salesperson to sell more efficiently with a higher likelihood of a sale.

THE ORGANIZATION OF THE BOOK

This book is organized into nine chapters. In Chapter 1, we lead off with a definition of market segmentation and its benefits. We follow up with a brief discussion about how business market segmentation differs from consumer segmentation. The chapter ends with an extensive discussion about alternative methods for segmenting business markets and criteria for evaluating segmentation methods. We conclude that needs-based segmentation offers practitioners significant advantages over alternative approaches.

Chapter 2 defines what we mean by *needs* and provides guidelines for operationalizing the concept of a need. We then talk about earlier efforts at needs segmentation, and we conclude with a discussion about the problems of identifying and measuring needs in a multiple decision-maker environment.

Chapter 3 presents our framework for segmenting business markets. We begin the chapter by identifying the principles that govern purchasing behaviors in business markets. We continue with a description of a multidimensional segmentation framework that incorporates the needs of significant domains of purchase influence. We conclude the chapter with an example of the framework in action.

Chapter 4 provides guidelines and lessons learned for conducting the market research necessary to identify needs and to segment business markets. Two phases of research are discussed, starting with the developmental qualitative research and followed by the quantification phase that uses survey research techniques. We finish this section with a discussion of various budget approaches to the research effort. The chapter concludes with a brief example of the use of the research data.

Chapter 5 explores the strategic applications of our needs-based segmentation approach. Among the applications we describe are market structure analysis, market selection and target markets, product portfolio value analysis, and competitive positioning. We wrap up the chapter with a discussion about the use of the framework as a strategic planning tool. Guidelines are offered for transitioning from strategic to tactical applications of the framework.

Chapter 6 presents a working description of tactical applications related to the marketing mix. These applications include tactical positioning, promotion advertising, distribution, and pricing.

Chapter 7 focuses on the design and implementation of a market information system as a critical vehicle for operationalizing a comprehensive needs-based approach to business markets. We begin the chapter with a definition of what we mean by a market information system complemented by a description of the benefits of installing such a system. We conclude the chapter with step-by-step guidelines for designing and operating a market information system.

Chapter 8 provides a framework and guidelines for implementing the approach. We start this chapter with a discussion of a holistic approach to implementation consisting of an information platform, analytic tools, and organizational environment guidelines. The section on organization focuses on techniques for addressing attitudinal barriers to implementation. We end the chapter with an important discussion about the critical contribution of cross-functional integration to successful implementation, including guidelines for using the approach in product development, marketing, and sales.

Finally, Chapter 9 uses a hypothetical case study to describe how a company pressured by competition can use all the elements of a market-driven, needs-based segmentation approach to produce and sustain a competitive advantage in the future.

SEGMENTATION MARKETING

1

THE BENEFITS OF USING MARKET-DRIVEN SEGMENTATION

AT&T's 800 phone service begins to experience fierce competition from MCI and US Sprint: For a variety of reasons, customers begin buying their 800 lines elsewhere, and AT&T needs to respond to protect its share. Realizing that some 800 service customers have developed more and more complex requirements as their usage has grown, AT&T recognizes the need for a range of offerings to appeal to different types of customers. In response, AT&T diversifies its 800 service, targeting customer needs that it feels AT&T can fill in a unique way, and simultaneously launches an aggressive marketing campaign to reach those target markets. Today AT&T offers three basic packages for 800 service with a myriad of options available in the high-end package. For AT&T, the marketing message is loud and clear: A single product is no longer sufficient for success.

In our many years of marketing experience across a broad

1

spectrum of industries and product categories, we have yet to find a market in which a single product appeals equally to all, or even most, customers. Such observations lead naturally to the "divide and rule" notion of market segmentation: namely, that maximum success results from thinking of your market as having different parts and attempting to serve those parts in different ways.

A multitude of approaches (most of them developed in consumer markets) have been used by marketers to implement this segmentation concept, and we will discuss many of them throughout this book. However, we will focus mainly on a particular approach called MBS — Market-driven Business Segmentation — that we have developed specifically to handle the increasing complexities of business-to-business markets in the 1990s.

To help you fully exploit the potential of MBS, we will offer practical advice on how to use our framework in the development and execution of business strategies. We will show you how MBS can be applied in analyzing and understanding the structure of your market, how it can guide your selection of product and service offerings, and how to use MBS in selecting target markets.

Strategy drives tactics — if it is a good strategy and is properly executed. MBS, being driven by customers' needs, yields powerful strategic direction and, to be most effective, should permeate most of your important tactical decision making. Consequently, we will also address applying MBS techniques to a number of tactical problems, such as the design of features for products and services, pricing, competitive positioning, advertising, promotion, and channel selection. And since MBS has implications for market information systems, we will touch on these as well.

As a first step in exploiting the MBS approach, this chapter will examine the concept of market segmentation, what motivates people to use it, and how it is currently approached in a business-to-business setting. We will also outline our vision of the way business market segmentation *should* be approached and the benefits it offers.

HOW BUSINESS MARKETING DIFFERS FROM CONSUMER MARKETING

Marketing to all but the smallest business customers is quite different from marketing to consumers. Without getting into specifics about what we mean by "small," we have generally found that the techniques for marketing to consumers and to small businesses are remarkably similar in most industries: both are mass markets widely dispersed geographically, with comparatively simple decision-making processes and more homogeneous needs than those of larger business customers.

In contrast, it is often necessary to sell directly to medium-to-large businesses, whose needs are much more diverse than are those of consumers or small businesses. This diversity is in part due to the fact that medium-to-large businesses tend to serve a broad variety of customers, but it is also because their product technology is often more complex and because these businesses have more complicated decision-making structures. In most instances, a number of individuals are involved in buying decisions, including purchasing agents, knowledgeable product users, financial officers, and senior management. In some cases — for example, computers, PBXs, or large heating and ventilation installations — customers also rely on the help of third-party consultants or specifiers who may actually make purchases on their behalf.

Despite their size and influence and the complexity of their markets, however, little attention has been given to market segmentation of medium-to-large businesses. It is these businesses that are the focus of this book, and, consequently, when we refer to "business customers," we are referring to medium-to-large businesses.

THE TRANSITION TO MARKET-DRIVEN DECISION MAKING

Business marketers confront a wide range of complex challenges (product development, marketing, sales, and so on) in their efforts to capture and expand market share. Quite understandably, it is not uncommon for them to seek solutions driven by the products and technologies with which they are familiar. All too often, however, such solutions prove to be inadequate or short lived.

Some time ago, for example, Alcoa decided to enter the aluminum bearing market. It based this market entry decision on two factors: compatibility with its existing manufacturing capabilities and the presence of the quality-control procedures needed to ensure a high-quality product. In other words, Alcoa decided to enter this market simply because it could — at least from a technical standpoint. As it turned out, Alcoa did not do well in this market, in part because it had entered without adequately assessing and responding to customers' needs.

As another example, consider the fact that, to date, most companies in the microcomputer industry have been highly product driven. When microcomputers were first widely introduced about 10 years ago, extensive marketing was not necessary: Good products virtually sold themselves. Today, with the market nearing saturation in many areas, the wise marketer must be concerned with adapting to user requirements for applications, superior service, and technical support

4

and with finding unexploited market niches. The old technology approach — "make 'em faster, bigger, and cheaper and they'll buy 'em" — will lead to extinction in the ongoing microcomputer market shakeout of the 1990s.

The previous examples illustrate two rules shaping business marketing today:

RULE 1: A MARKET-DRIVEN STRATEGY IS ESSENTIAL.

In a competitive market, it is essential that a company examine and respond to the needs of its customers in making key business decisions. While responsiveness to customer needs is integral to consumer marketing, it does not appear to be a common practice among business marketers, perhaps because both business products and the customers who buy them are so much more complex. *Of course* it is important for your company to possess relevant technology and to understand the products competing in your markets. However, to put it bluntly, if your corporate strategy and product planning are not driven by the demands of your customers, then you will not be as successful as you could be for as long as you could be.

RULE 2: THINK OF YOUR CUSTOMERS AS COMING IN MANY FLAVORS.

The assortment of customer needs readily observed in the marketplace requires such a perspective. It is possible to take this point of view to extremes, treating every customer as a unique market, requiring a unique product. The proliferation of options in business telephone service, with virtually every customer having its own customized phone system, is an obvious example of this. As the Japanese auto industry has shown, however, sometimes there are benefits to avoiding the excessive cost of developing so many unique products and of supporting them once they are in place. Market segmentation offers an effective compromise between the two extremes of ignoring customer differences and treating every customer as unique.

USING SEGMENTATION TO ADDRESS BUSINESS MARKETING PROBLEMS

Simply put, market segmentation is the division of customers into groups. These groups can be (and have been) selected based on a number of factors, but usually we want the groups to differ in one or more important characteristics relevant to their purchase or usage behaviors. To be effective, segmentation must not be too complicated to understand and use effectively; at the same time it must capture the diversity of the customer population being targeted.

An example of a straightforward segmentation is one based on geography, in which customers are divided according to sales territories. To the extent that there are regional differences in purchase or usage, this may be a useful segmentation; typically, however, this approach is based on administrative convenience and is not directly related to purchase or usage patterns. As a result, we can often find a better basis for segmentation than geography.

A somewhat more useful example of segmentation is offered by the "demand classes" used by the electric utility industry (a demand class is a grouping of customers based on their peak usage of electricity during the month). Presumably, customers with similar patterns of electricity usage have similar needs regarding the quality of service from their utility. This segmentation is better than one based on service territory (geography) alone because it reflects customer behaviors that the utility can use to manage electricity demand. However, can we really expect Kmart and an office complex — two customers with similar electricity demands — to respond similarly to marketing and product offerings? Almost certainly not.

Clearly, segmentations based on geography or usage can be valuable. We feel strongly that such bases for segmentation do provide helpful information that a careful marketer can take advantage of in designing the strategy and tactics for a marketing plan. But it is also true that such bases for segmentation have serious shortcomings, many of which we will explore later in this chapter.

Despite the limitations of the approaches outlined above, marketers have a variety of marketing questions that skillful segmentation techniques can help them answer. A good segmentation strategy must provide answers to several key questions — referred to later as the "Four Q's" (see Exhibit 2).

Exhibit 2
MARKETING QUESTIONS ADDRESSED BY SEGMENTATION
(THE FOUR Q's)

QUESTIONS	ISSUES	ACTIVITIES AFFECTED
WHAT?	WHAT PRODUCTS AND SERVICES TO OFFER	STRATEGIC PLANNING, PRODUCT DEVELOPMENT, MARKETING, PRICING
WHO?	AT WHOM TO AIM PRODUCTS AND SERVICES	SALES, ADVERTISING, MARKETING
WHERE?	WHERE TO ADVERTISE AND MARKET	ADVERTISING, MARKETING
WHY?	WHY CUSTOMERS DO WHAT THEY DO	ALL

- **What?** What products and services to offer? The answer to this question is at the heart of planning your business strategy: It affects product development, pricing, and positioning. What features should your products and services offer? How should they be priced? What incentives (such as rebates, free trials, free technical consulting) should you offer to stimulate purchase? Which product or service features should be emphasized in your merchandising program?

- **Who?** At whom should you aim your products and services? Which customers will be most responsive? What are their identifying characteristics from a marketing perspective? Who are the key influencers in the purchase decision? A successful answer to these questions will guide not only your sales efforts, but your choice of distribution channels as well.

- **Where?** What vehicles represent the best means of promoting your products and services? Is a national TV advertising campaign appropriate for a business-to-business product or would direct mail be more effective? What trade journals do your customers read? Are telemarketing efforts appropriate?

- **Why?** Why should customers buy your products and services instead of something else? What motivates them to make purchases in the first place? How can you shape your products and marketing to appeal to whatever drives the customers you want to reach?

In our view, the *Why?* question has the broadest implications for segmentation. If we truly understand what motivates our customers, we already know a lot about *who* they are, *what* products and services they want, and *where* to reach them.

In fact, we would define a market-driven company as one that understands why its customers do what they do. When a company understands the *Why* behind its customers' decisions, the implications for its business success cut across all its functions and activities, from strategic planning through product development through pricing, marketing, and sales. Thus, while all four marketing questions are important, the last one is by far the most significant.

In the next section, we examine a number of traditional approaches to business market segmentation in light of a number of criteria. Chief among them is their effectiveness in answering the *Why?* question that drives customer behavior.

TRADITIONAL SEGMENTATION APPROACHES

Having decided to adopt a segmentation approach, marketers are confronted with the problem of which one to use. As noted earlier, there are many traditional approaches in current use, all of which vary in terms of the customer characteristics used as the basis for segmentation. Analytic methods used to divide customers into segments also vary widely. We will not discuss these methods here since they are described in many good textbooks on statistics or research methods — and because, in our view, the value of an approach depends far more on customer characteristics and how they are captured than on analytic techniques. This is not to say that analysis issues are unimportant. They can be quite critical in implementing a segmentation strategy, but the method should be dictated by the segmentation model adopted — not the reverse.

Traditional business segmentation approaches can be categorized into four general classes based on the key customer characteristics used: firmographics, decision-making unit characteristics, usage, and products.

Firmographic Segmentation

Firmographics are analogous to demographics for consumers: They are easily verified, objective characteristics of a business.

9

The geographic service territory segmentation mentioned earlier is an example of a firmographic segmentation.

Business size measures — such as number of employees, gross revenues, and number of locations — are often used as firmographic segmentation devices to divide customers into segments. Our small versus medium-to-large customers discussion earlier is a rough example of size segmentation. Most telephone operating companies and long-distance carriers divide their customers into National or Priority Accounts (very large customers), Major Accounts (medium-sized customers), and General Business Accounts (small businesses), to whom they market and service quite differently.

Standard Industrial Classification (SIC) codes are another popular form of firmographic segmentation. SIC codes are an exhaustive set of business categories created by the U.S. Office of Management and Budget to reflect the economic activities of all businesses and government agencies in the United States. The broadest level of SIC codes divides organizations into 11 divisions as shown in Exhibit 3. These broad divisions are further subdivided into a total of 84 major groups (also referred to as the "two-digit codes"). The two-digit codes are in turn subdivided into three- and then four-digit codes at even greater levels of detail, for a total of 1005 SIC codes.

Many businesses find SIC codes a convenient segmentation tool for organizing marketing, sales, service, and product development activities, because SICs reflect the nature of businesses and thus, presumably, of the products and services they acquire.

Assigning businesses to SIC codes can be somewhat problematic in that many companies (even divisions within companies) belong to more than one code. Conglomerates are often in more than one SIC division. Many Fortune 500 companies are difficult to classify. For example, while Procter &

Exhibit 3
SIC CODES

DIVISIONS	NO. OF TWO-DIGIT CODES	NO. OF THREE-DIGIT CODES	NO. OF FOUR-DIGIT CODES
A. AGRICULTURE, FORESTRY, AND FISHING	5	23	58
B. MINING	4	20	31
C. CONSTRUCTION	3	14	26
D. MANUFACTURING	20	140	459
E. TRANSPORTATION AND PUBLIC UTILITIES	10	37	67
F. WHOLESALE TRADE	2	18	69
G. RETAIL TRADE	8	41	64
H. FINANCE, INSURANCE, AND REAL ESTATE	8	30	53
I. SERVICES	16	71	150
J. PUBLIC ADMINISTRATION	7	21	27
K. NONCLASSIFIABLE ESTABLISHMENTS	1	1	1

Gamble belongs in the Manufacturing Division, it can be assigned to 3 different two-digit codes, at least 10 three-digit codes, and 19 four-digit codes. Many locations within Procter & Gamble (e.g., General Offices or the Technical Centers) would also be assigned to multiple four-, three-, and even two-digit codes.

Combinations of firmographics are also popular. Perhaps the most common form of firmographic segmentation is SIC crossed with size, as shown in Exhibit 4.

Presumably, large establishments in one SIC division will have similar needs and purchasing patterns and will differ from establishments in other divisions.

Decision-making Unit (DMU) Segmentation

DMU is a common acronym referring to that part of an organization that makes decisions about which products and services

Exhibit 4
FIRMOGRAPHIC SEGMENTATION EXAMPLE

SIC CODES	SIZE (NO. OF EMPLOYEES)		
	<1000	1000 TO 9999	10,000+
A. AGRICULTURE, FORESTRY, AND FISHING			
B. MINING			
C. CONSTRUCTION			
D. MANUFACTURING			
E. TRANSPORTATION AND PUBLIC UTILITIES			
F. WHOLESALE TRADE			
G. RETAIL TRADE			
H. FINANCE, INSURANCE, AND REAL ESTATE			
I. SERVICES			
J. PUBLIC ADMINISTRATION			
K. NONCLASSIFIABLE ESTABLISHMENTS			

to buy. Obviously, different parts of an organization may be responsible for different purchasing decisions. DMU segmentation, unlike firmographic segmentation, requires a focus only on DMUs with responsibility for purchasing a particular product or service category.

DMU segmentation is based on organizational characteristics that reflect the complexity of the decision-making process. Thus, for example, DMUs characterized by centralized decision making often have very different needs to satisfy and require a different selling process from those required by DMUs with decentralized decision-making processes.

Other common DMU segmentations are based on the number of influencers in the decision process (e.g., a single decision maker versus multiple decision makers) and on the organizational roles of the influencers. For example, a purchase of manufacturing supplies made solely on spec through a purchasing agent is very different from one of a computer network in which systems managers, end users, senior management, and even third-party consultants all have some degree of influence over the final outcome.

DMU segmentation is usually motivated by the sales function, where it has its greatest direct value. Also, sales reps often provide the data needed to assign customers to DMU segments. Unlike firmographic segmentation, assignment of a customer to a DMU segment cannot be based only on publicly available information: Knowledge of the inner workings and structure of the customer's organization is required, and sales reps often have that knowledge. Of course, it must be admitted that this is only the reps' perception — and not necessarily the reality — of what can be a complex internal process.

Usage-based Segmentation

Usage in this context refers to customer behaviors influencing any element of use of a product or service. This can include either initial purchase or ongoing use. It can also include use of your product or of a portfolio of your products and those of your competitors.

Typically, usage-based segments are similar to size-based firmographic segments, except that, in this case, size means volume of purchases. For example, consider again the demand classes used by most electric utilities for segmenting their commercial and industrial customers. *Demand* is defined as the peak amount of electricity used by a customer in a month, with heavy industry and large government establishments tending to fall into the highest demand class. Not surprisingly, the distribution of customers across the demand classes is skewed, with relatively few in the higher classes and enormous numbers in the lower classes.

A related but slightly different variation involves defining segments in terms of usage in general, not just usage of your product. Note that in the demand class example above, such a segmentation does not incorporate overall usage of competing energy sources (e.g., fossil fuels) or usage of electricity from other generators (e.g., from utilities in other parts of the country or from cogeneration, the production of electricity as a by-product of some other operation, such as manufacturing). A more general usage segmentation, covering competitors' offerings as well as your own firm's, is more useful for competitive strategy or product and service planning.

Usage-based segmentation can be more complex than these two examples suggest. Marketers have used purchase situations, such as initial purchase versus straight replacement versus upgrade, to segment customers. They have also used distinct purchase or usage patterns over time as a basis for segmenting customers. For example, electric utilities usually have load profiles on their customers detailing the amount of electricity being used at each of a series of points in time, across a day, week, or month. Groups of customers with different load profiles can be identified. Such an analysis is frequently undertaken for engineering purposes, but is rarely used by utilities as a basis for organizing marketing activities.

Product-based Segmentation

Products or their characteristics (here *product* refers to either a product or service) may also be used as a basis for segmentation. As with usage-based segmentation, this approach can focus either on your products exclusively, or it can include competitive product offerings.

It is common to divide the world into users and nonusers of your product or products. Identifying the characteristics that distinguish users from nonusers can be very helpful in sales, selection of distribution channels, advertising, and positioning. A somewhat richer approach involves segmenting customers based on the portfolio of products they purchase or own in each product category. For example, communications system vendors sometimes group their customers based on the kinds of networks they already have in place. Or computer manufacturers' customers may be segmented according to their installed base of workstations, terminals, servers, and processors.

Finally, a very useful product segmentation is based on product features. Dividing customers into segments that differ based on the features they are seeking begins to tap deeper into customer value systems. When US West used this approach as the basis for a metropolitan-area network offering, it was able to identify opportunities for several different network packages.

Combinations of these traditional segmentation bases can be used quite effectively. We have seen DMU and usage-based approaches used together: each of a number of purchase situations (first purchase, replacement, and so on) separating each of several DMU types (e.g., centralized versus decentralized decisions). Each combination of purchase situation and DMU types exhibits somewhat different purchase behaviors and merits a different set of marketing positionings, product and service offerings, channels, and so on.

The four traditional segmentation bases described above distribute themselves in an obvious way along a market-driven versus product-driven continuum as illustrated in Exhibit 5. While the first two types of segmentation, firmographic and DMU, focus on customer characteristics (and hence are market driven), product-based segmentation lies at the other extreme and usage-based segmentation falls somewhere in the middle.

Exhibit 5
CONTINUUM OF SEGMENTATION BASES

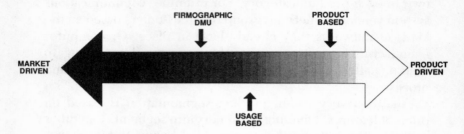

Note however, that things are not as clear as they might seem at first blush. None of these forms of segmentation are extreme examples of either end of the continuum. Compared to a focus only on technology with no regard to customer characteristics at all (as illustrated in the Alcoa example), product-based segmentation is at least somewhat concerned with customer behavior. Furthermore, product *feature*-based segmentation (as illustrated by the US West example) is actually very much concerned with the needs of the customer. On the other hand, the two types of segmentation on the market-driven side are not strongly market driven according to our earlier definition: responsiveness to customer needs. Neither firmographics nor DMU segmentation directly assesses customer needs as a part of the marketing process.

It is natural for all of us to try to keep our lives as simple as possible, and so most first attempts at segmentation are fairly straightforward geographic- or user versus nonuser-based schemes. In fact, the most common reason we hear for adopting a segmentation approach is: "It was an easy one to apply." Certainly, ease of application is important — if a segmentation is too complex, it won't be used. However, skillful marketers

16

quickly discover that simplicity is not the only criterion — nor is it the best one.

EVALUATING TRADITIONAL APPROACHES TO SEGMENTATION

Based on many years of working in this area, we have developed what we believe to be a complete list of nine criteria for evaluating the relative strengths and weaknesses of traditional segmentation approaches.

CRITERION 1: THE FOUR Q'S

The more successfully a segmentation provides answers to the four "what, who, where, and why" marketing questions that we discussed earlier, the more valuable the segmentation will be. It also goes without saying that if everyone in your organization has the same perspective on your market, speaks the same language, and has a common framework for developing both corporate strategy and tactics, then your business will run more smoothly, in a more unified and focused fashion, and you will be more successful in the long run. Since the four marketing questions cover so much territory, a segmentation that answers them will provide a unifying perspective on the market across functions in your organization. In fact, we believe that the best segmentation structure is one that has enough depth and universality to provide that perspective.

CRITERION 2: ACTIONABILITY

The most elegant segmentation in the world is superfluous if it is never used to make business decisions.

Therefore, a segmentation must be judged by the extent to which it can be used as the basis for practical decisions. This is partly an efficiency issue: The more a segmentation can be used, the more productive your company will be. But actionability is also a matter of breadth of coverage across different functions within your organization, which relates back to the "unifying perspective" discussed above: The best segmentation provides you with a rational basis for organizing your entire company.

CRITERION 3: ACCESSIBILITY

A segmentation must divide customers in a way that makes it possible to identify and reach them through your marketing and selling efforts. If it does not, then the segments are inaccessible. Accessibility may be achieved either directly (as in the case of geographic segmentation) or by reference to reachable customer characteristics. For example, electric utility demand classes (usage-based segments) are accessible because the utility has very accurate records of actual usage for each and every customer. But such is often not the case with usage-based segments. Computer manufacturers, for example, find it difficult to know in detail exactly how much computing with each brand of computer is actually performed by all their business customers. Consequently, segments based on computer usage by themselves are not directly accessible without more information than can be obtained from sales records about customers in different segments.

CRITERION 4: VOLUME AND USAGE

To be relevant, a good segmentation must identify customer segments that differ at least to some extent in their gross product category behaviors, such as volume of purchases or amount of product usage. If segments do not show some differences in volume or usage, then it is questionable whether the characteristics used as the basis for that segmentation are related to customer behaviors. Given acceptable differences between segments, volume and usage become criteria for selecting segments to target against for marketing and selling. Those segments with the biggest revenue potential due to high volume and usage become attractive targets, their attractiveness being modified, of course, by our ability to meet their needs uniquely and by the cost of doing so with winning products and services.

CRITERION 5: GLOBALISM

This term refers to the utility of a segmentation approach across global markets. If your company competes (or would like to compete) in international markets, any segmentation approach you use must be adaptable across national boundaries. For example, SIC codes, based as they are on the U.S. economy, may not apply to third-world markets. If a segmentation approach is not easily adapted to different countries, you will suffer the confusion and inefficiencies of fragmented strategies and bear the cost of reinventing a unique segmentation in each country.

CRITERION 6: DURABILITY

This criterion refers to the question of how stable customer segments are over time. We refer here to stability in the nature of the segments, not in their size. Segments grow and shrink over time as businesses are born, grow, and fail. However, if this occurs too rapidly, the segments completely disappear, and new ones spring up in a short time frame, making it impossible to formulate a strategy that will stay current. Segmentations based on brand usage in a rapidly changing market generally prove to be short lived and nondurable.

Criterion 7: Face Validity

This criterion is simply an appeal to common sense: Does the segmentation appear to be intuitively sensible on the face of it? For instance, it makes sense that large businesses in the Manufacturing SIC division need different ventilating systems than medium-sized companies in the Retail Trade category. The more logical a segmentation appears to marketers, the more likely it is to be used. Conversely, if a segmentation approach is too counter-intuitive, it will not be used, *even if it is right*.

Criterion 8: Replicability

A segmentation structure that assigns customers to segments the same way, no matter who does the analyses or which customers are being assigned, is also much more effective than one that does not. Most segmentations are replicable in this sense. However, this is not true when a segmentation is based on subjective data, particularly when the data come from someone besides the customers themselves. For example, if, in a DMU segmentation, your sales reps provide you with the data, the results are less likely to be reproducible because different reps have different levels of understanding of their customers. A DMU segmentation is most likely to be replicable if the data for it come directly from customers.

CRITERION 9: MULTIDIMENSIONALITY

In a way, this criterion is also an appeal to common sense, as is Criterion 7 (Face Validity): It acknowledges that business markets are complicated. There are many dimensions on which business customers' behaviors are influenced, ranging from easily observed dimensions such as geographic location to intangibles such as product features sought. Those segmentations that capture complexity will tend to be the most powerful. Two simple examples are the segmentation shown in Exhibit 4, SIC by employee size, and the segmentation using purchase situation by DMU types discussed on pages 11–13. Both examples show more useful multidimensional segmentations than do any of the individual dimensions alone (i.e., SIC, employee size, purchase situation, or DMU type). This is a fundamental characteristic of our MBS approach, which we will illustrate in greater detail later.

With these nine criteria in mind, we can evaluate the four traditional bases for segmentation, as illustrated in Exhibit 6. In an exercise of this sort, of course, there is some subjectivity involved, and there are always instances that can be cited as counterexamples to any judgments we have made. However, Exhibit 6 does reflect our experience with these four approaches as we have seen them typically practiced.

So how well are marketers being served by the traditional approaches to segmentation? On the whole, the answer is "only moderately well." In terms of some criteria — Face Validity, the *Who?* question, and Replicability — traditional approaches are effective. However, these are relatively easy criteria to meet, either explicitly or with a little extra effort.

21

Some very important criteria are not being met well at all. The criterion previously identified as most important, namely the *Why?* question, is not being addressed well by any approach. Multidimensionality, admittedly a difficult criterion to meet (but important nonetheless), is also being addressed poorly. And the *What?* and *Where?* questions are also being answered inadequately, depending on the approach used.

To the extent that answering the Four Q's is essential to becoming more market driven, traditional segmentation approaches are weak. Given the importance of the *Why?*

Exhibit 6
EVALUATION OF THE FOUR TRADITIONAL SEGMENTATIONS

CRITERIA	FIRMO-GRAPHIC	DMU	USAGE BASED	PRODUCT BASED
1. THE 4 QUESTIONS:				
WHAT?	○	○	○	●
WHO?	●	●	◐	●
WHERE?	◐	◐	○	○
WHY?	○	○	○	○
2. ACTIONABILITY	◐	◐	◐	◐
3. ACCESSIBILITY	●	◐	◐	◐
4. VOLUME AND USAGE	◐	○	●	◐
5. GLOBALISM	◐	●	◐	◐
6. DURABILITY	○	○	●	○
7. FACE VALIDITY	●	●	●	●
8. REPLICABILITY	●	◐	●	●
9. MULTIDIMENSIONALITY	○	○	○	○
OVERALL	◐	◐	◐	◐

○ CANNOT MEET CRITERION WITHOUT SIGNIFICANT AUGMENTATION
◐ MEETS CRITERION PARTIALLY OR WITH SOME AUGMENTATION
● MEETS CRITERION EXPLICITLY

question to market-driven companies, the four traditional approaches clearly offer inadequate support.

In consumer products industries, when confronted by similar problems, marketers have turned to some form of needs-based analysis, ranging from preferences to attitudes to lifestyles, from physical deficits to personality traits. Just as an individual consumer's product and brand usage is in response to his or her needs regarding the relevant category, so an organization's behavior is responsive to the needs that drive its management and employees — needs that may be economic, structural, functional, or fundamental values of the corporate culture. Needs can be thought of as explicit answers to the *Why?* question. To answer the *Why?* question in the business context, we must extend the consumer product industries' approaches to the business marketing world.

THE MARKET-DRIVEN SEGMENTATION VISION

Because the business customer is so much more complex than an individual consumer, segmentation methods used to reach consumers just do not transfer easily: In our experience, a laundry list of individual customer needs is usually too oversimplified and misses one or more important components of the business customer decision-making process.

In the market-driven business segmentation (MBS) approach, we use a series of assumptions. These assumptions are thoroughly explored in Chapter 3, but it may be useful here to give a brief overview of the approach.

In common with consumer needs segmentation, MBS assumes that needs precede behavior. That is, if we understand the needs that drive our business customers, then we have the fundamental basis for understanding and influencing our markets.

However, in contrast to the consumer market, a business customer is actually a multiplicity of organizational levels. Different levels and functions within the purchasing organization attempt to meet their needs relative to a particular product or service category by influencing purchase decisions in different ways. There are usually several levels of influence affecting major purchase decisions: Often, the larger the company, the more levels. These levels include senior management with its strategic and policy concerns, the manager of the function most relevant to the product and service category (usually the purchaser) with specific operational and logistical needs, and the end users of the product or service with their very practical and immediate day-to-day needs. Notice that these levels and their associated needs carry with them an implicit hierarchical ordering within the purchasing organization, usually based on their importance and the relevance of the category to their sphere of responsibility.

In MBS, we therefore segment on the basis of a formal hierarchy of organizational needs — strategic, operational, functional, and so on — reflecting the above assumptions. Not all customers are unique in their hierarchy of needs. There are groups of customers who share common needs, which leads to the possibility of segmenting customers.

Of course, needs by themselves are not sufficient to fully explain customer purchasing behavior: Other factors such as short-term cash flow, distribution channel barriers, and regulatory environments are also important constraints on the decision process. Consequently, the MBS approach attempts to factor in these constraints as well.

Since we began with the nine criteria shown in Exhibit 6, we purposefully set out with MBS to correct what we believed to be shortcomings of the traditional approaches without any significant "give-ups." At this point, since we haven't really described MBS, you will have to accept our evaluation of MBS in Exhibit 7 as an expression of our objectives in this approach. By the time you have finished with this book, we believe you will agree with this evaluation.

With some augmentation of the data intrinsic to a needs segmentation, MBS can satisfy all nine criteria. In particular, the all-important *Why?* question is answered extremely well by MBS, since we obtain a great deal of information about what motivates customers to make purchases. And, by using MBS to identify the hierarchy of needs at different organizational levels, we capture Multidimensionality as well. The other bases for our judgments in Exhibit 7 should become apparent as we explain MBS in greater detail.

Exhibit 7
**EVALUATION OF THE TRADITIONAL SEGMENTATIONS *AND*
THE MBS APPROACH**

CRITERIA	FIRMO-GRAPHIC	DMU	USAGE BASED	PRODUCT BASED	MBS
1. THE 4 QUESTIONS:					
WHAT?	○	○	○	●	●
WHO?	●	●	◐	●	●
WHERE?	◐	◐	○	○	◐
WHY?	○	○	○	○	◐
2. ACTIONABILITY	◐	◐	◐	◐	●
3. ACCESSIBILITY	●	●	◐	◐	◐
4. VOLUME AND USAGE	◐	○	●	◐	◐
5. GLOBALISM	◐	●	◐	◐	◐
6. DURABILITY	○	○	◐	○	●
7. FACE VALIDITY	●	●	●	●	●
8. REPLICABILITY	●	◐	●	●	●
9. MULTIDIMENSIONALITY	○	○	○	○	●
OVERALL	◐	◐	◐	◐	●

○ CANNOT MEET CRITERION WITHOUT SIGNIFICANT AUGMENTATION
◐ MEETS CRITERION PARTIALLY OR WITH SOME AUGMENTATION
● MEETS CRITERION EXPLICITLY

25

Notice that, despite our obvious enthusiasm for our approach, we do not believe MBS will meet all of your needs as a business marketer. In fact, we feel that other approaches can be used to augment the MBS approach. MBS does not necessarily eliminate the usefulness of existing segmentation approaches. Rather, we see it as an overlay to traditional approaches and as a fundamental organizing principle for your business.

Clearly, traditional approaches are often useful or even necessary. For example, MBS's primary weaknesses lie in two related areas: the *Where?* question and the Accessibility criterion. Firmographics and DMU characteristics are useful supplements to MBS segments to buttress this gap. MBS should not be thought of as eliminating the need for traditional information sources, but rather as correcting important shortcomings and providing a widely applicable basis for conducting your business.

Most important, adopting MBS provides you with a thorough understanding of your customers' characteristics and motivations. If you act on that understanding, you are, by definition, market driven. MBS will carry you closer to the market-driven ideal than any other segmentation approach, as illustrated in Exhibit 8.

Exhibit 8
CONTINUUM OF SEGMENTATION BASES WITH MBS

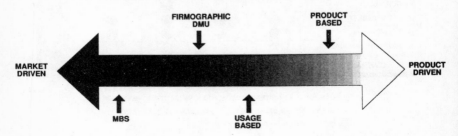

The Benefits of Using Market-driven Segmentation

Past efforts at segmenting business markets on the basis of needs have not always worked well in practice because of the inherent complexity of the purchase decision-making process and difficulties in applying the results of business market segmentation to real-world business decisions. Therefore, before fully exploring the MBS approach, we will describe more about how needs are identified in the business context, about needs-based approaches to segmentation, and about some critical problems in implementing these approaches.

2

CUSTOMER NEEDS AS THE BASIS OF A MARKET-DRIVEN APPROACH

THE MEANING OF *NEEDS*

The word *needs* means different things to different people. In our review of marketing literature and in our discussions with other marketers, we find examples of needs that are all over the map. To name just a few, people attempt to measure (and market to) needs in terms of

- specific branded products desired (e.g., Intel 80286 or Motorola 68000 microchips)
- manufacturer preferred (e.g., Xerox or Kodak)
- specific product features needed (e.g., communications line bandwidth, shipment delivery time)
- product-servicing requirements (e.g., availability of 800 number for technical support, billing detail)

- decision-making styles (e.g., need for certainty, speed of decision making)
- corporate policies (e.g., centralization of decisions, level of cash flow)
- corporate styles (e.g., innovativeness, customer orientation)

In the most general terms, *needs* are defined as internal conditions that motivate the use of a particular product or service. Needs are not external to the customer: They must be internal, or they are not really needs. For instance, we do not usually refer to factors in the economic environment as needs (although a business can have a need to respond to changes in economic, competitive, or regulatory environments).

This is not to say that external forces do not influence customer behaviors. On the contrary, constraints are imposed on behavior by the environment in which the customer is operating. The economic, competitive, or regulatory climates, for example, are situational constraints that limit or shape the customer's options. Or, as another example, distribution problems can make some products or services unavailable. Furthermore, external factors may facilitate behaviors. For example, MCI and Sprint benefit greatly from regulatory actions restricting AT&T's pricing policies.

In fact, some needs can be thought of as the customer's response to, or strategies for, dealing with situational constraints. A need for liquidity or a willingness to incur debt may be as much a response to how well the economy is doing as it is to the state of the individual customer's business — or it may just be corporate style.

Motivation is a significant component of the definition of needs. There is always a causal aspect to a need: It is something in the customer that drives purchase and usage behaviors. Needs are therefore very informative: If we understand needs

29

in the context of situational constraints, then by definition, we understand why customers do what they do and many of the key considerations in their actions. In fact, customers' needs should be thought of as the factors that would completely determine their choices if no external situational constraints limited their decisions. There must also be a degree of importance in needs, an element of priority. If something is not important to a customer, then it will not motivate purchase or use.

By our definition, needs are separate and distinct from such factors as behaviors or product features or other customer characteristics that are not directly motivational. This may seem obvious, but we have seen many instances in which product features or firmographics have been described as though they were actually needs. Obviously, the SIC of a customer is not itself a need. Although we might guess about the needs of customers based on the fact that they are in, say, the wholesale trade, we cannot really know what those needs are, nor should we expect all wholesalers in a particular product category to have the same needs.

As another example, the customer's product purchases represent a behavior of that customer, yet only indirectly reflect the customer's needs. The knowledge that a company buys Novell netware with IBM PS/2 Model 50 and 70 workstations (a series of behaviors), for example, is not really enough for us to be able to infer why those products are purchased (the underlying needs) — only that they were purchased. Different customers often buy the same software and hardware for fundamentally different reasons. One company might buy Novell and IBM because it recognizes its own lack of expertise and does not want to take any chances while at the same time it does not want to make the kind of investment it would take to acquire that kind of expertise. Another firm might buy the same products because its exhaustive technical evaluation of all options indicates that the Novell and IBM combination is the most reliable and will best meet all of its technical needs. Yet another customer might buy the same products because it needs good technical support from vendors and believes Novell and IBM offer the best service. Another, because it is corporate policy to deal only with those specific vendors.

The point is that purchase behavior and purchase motivation are not synonymous and should not be confused. While purchase behavior might reflect motivations and might provide useful customer data for a variety of purposes, that information does not serve all of the same objectives as do needs.

A more subtle issue arises with respect to product or service features. As with product purchase, it can be invaluable (particularly for product development) to understand customer preferences for specific product features, but once again, this does not serve the same purpose as understanding the underlying needs driving those preferences. Consider a data communications example: A customer purchases a particular kind of dedicated line. Imagine asking a series of *Why?* questions such as the following.

"Why did you buy that?"
  "Because it best meets our needs."   (a nonanswer)
"Why do you think that?"
  "Because it had the right
  bandwidth for us."   (a product feature)
"Why did you want that bandwidth?"
  "Because we need to transmit
  extremely large files twice a day
  and the transmission must be
  completed very quickly."   (a need)
"Why . . . ?"

31

This line of questioning continues until you start getting vague answers like "Because we want to be successful." In a sense, every answer the customer gives to the *Why?* questions reveals a different level of need. One could certainly argue that the customer has a "need for a certain bandwidth," and finding what it is would be a useful thing to know. But that is not the level of need that we would find most useful: It reflects a product-driven approach and, as discussed in Chapter 1, is therefore limited in its ability to meet several of the criteria for segmentation success. The next level of need, the need to transmit data in certain ways, is more widely applicable across functions in your company (not limited to product development), is more durable over time than are the specific bandwidths preferred, and is more causal in nature relative to choice between alternatives. It also reveals more about customer motivations and could help you better tailor service for that customer. Understanding that this customer occasionally needs to quickly move large amounts of data suggests requirements for line reliability and baud rates that are different from the need to move moderate amounts of data continuously. Note that in both cases the bandwidth preferred might be exactly the same.

On the other hand, we believe that there is some level of need beyond which it is not fruitful to proceed. Certainly, knowing that a customer ultimately wants to buy data communications lines "because we want to be successful" is not very useful. This level is so basic and nondiscriminating that it does not suggest much at all about what customers will consider buying to meet that need, something that the product feature level does so well. In fact, we would argue that the best level of needs at which to operate is that which strikes the best balance between *what* the customer wants and *why* the customer wants it — in the present example, the "need to move some volume of data at a specific frequency" is better than either "bandwidth" (what) at one extreme or "to be successful" (why) at the other. Finding this balance point can be difficult and is part of the art of the needs-based approach to marketing.

To summarize, needs are internal conditions that motivate customers' purchase or use of products and services. Needs are *not* such things as behaviors or other nonmotivating or non-differentiating customer characteristics. Product feature preferences are close to needs but are expressed at a level that is not as informative as we would like about why customers do what they do.

IS IT POSSIBLE TO IDENTIFY
THE NEEDS OF A BUSINESS?

The answer is an emphatic "Yes!" How do you do that? Go ask customers. We recognize that assessing needs in a business setting is very difficult. The fact that there are often a number of purchasing agents as well as a number of important purchase influencers with different needs creates problems on two fronts: in collecting the data and in the fact that there are a variety of needs. In addition, there is a serious question surrounding the very measurement of business needs: Since needs are less tangible than, say, firmographics such as SIC or number of employees, how can needs be measured reliably?

Multiple Decision Makers: Data Collection

To reflect the needs in different relevant parts of an organization, you may need to determine the perspective of more than one person. This is in marked contrast to consumer products categories in which a single person is normally the purchaser and can at least reflect accurately the needs of others (e.g., other household members) involved in the purchase. Since you do not fully know the needs of a company unless the perspectives of all interested parties are represented, you may need to gather data from all the people who are important influencers on the decision. Bearing in mind that we are restricting our attention in this book to medium-to-large companies, it would be desirable to interview, if possible, at least two types of individuals per establishment to complete data collection: usually someone from senior management with overall strategic responsibilities for the business unit targeted by the product and someone knowledgeable about the target business unit or function. For instance, in a study of transoceanic shipping, we would like to interview both the VP of Operations and the shipping manager, the former as the best representative of corporate strategy and general business objectives and the latter for the functional knowledge about how the company actually uses the product. Each person should be interviewed only about the business needs he or she knows best and is responsible for meeting.

Multiple Decision Makers: Variety of Needs

In addition to the logistical difficulties of interviewing more than one person, the number of decision makers involved also tends to multiply the sheer number of needs that must be measured. In the transoceanic shipping example, the complex strategic and general operations needs that the VP of Operations identifies must be layered on top of the functional and product-specific needs of the shipping manager. This alone creates difficulties in data collection, preparation, and analysis. The discipline of some theoretical framework is absolutely necessary to prevent information overload and to provide a structure for understanding how decisions are made and for acting on the information gathered. This framework is fully described in Chapter 3.

Reliable Needs Measurement

The variety of needs present in the market varies in terms of importance and magnitude. To establish the extent to which needs are present among your customers requires that we measure those needs in some systematic way. Measurement of needs allows us to prioritize them. Fortunately, business needs may be measured using the same techniques that are applied in consumer products categories to ensure reliable measurement. Essentially, these are the techniques of attitude measurement that are described in detail in any of a number of textbooks on the subject.

Briefly, we measure needs by asking decision makers to react to a series of statements. Several such statements are illustrated in Exhibit 9. These statements represent needs in a language and terminology used by the decision makers themselves. Typically, though not always, the decision makers indicate the degree to which they feel the statement represents their organization, using an "agree/disagree" rating scale such as that shown in Exhibit 9.

But ratings of individual statements are notoriously unreliable: Repeated ratings by the same individuals show substantial inconsistency. This inconsistency is like the noise obscuring a signal we wish to detect — in this case, the signal is the underlying need. Any individual statement measures the need we wish to assess to some degree, but it also is measuring other things as well: related needs or attitudes, product perceptions, and even such unrelated things as vocabulary skills. In addition, some of the noise is simply random variation in responses by an individual in judging the needs of the organization. It is possible to eliminate much of this inconsistency

Exhibit 9
SAMPLE NEEDS STATEMENTS AND RATINGS

	STRONGLY DISAGREE	DISAGREE	SLIGHTLY DISAGREE	SLIGHTLY AGREE	AGREE	STRONGLY AGREE
TO BE COMPETITIVE, OUR ORGANIZATION IS WILLING TO TAKE RISKS	1	2	3	4	5	6
IN OUR ORGANIZATION, LONG-RANGE PLANNING IS CRITICAL TO MAKING PRUDENT DAY-TO-DAY BUSINESS DECISIONS	1	2	3	4	5	6
OUR ORGANIZATION LIKES TO RELY ON NEW TECHNOLOGIES TO SOLVE PROBLEMS	1	2	3	4	5	6
OUR MANAGEMENT IS WILLING TO TAKE RISKS TO GROW THE BUSINESS MORE RAPIDLY	1	2	3	4	5	6
WE NEED TO BE ON THE LEADING EDGE OF NEW TECHNOLOGY TO BE SUCCESSFUL	1	2	3	4	5	6
IN OUR ORGANIZATION WE NEED TO APPLY RIGOROUS FINANCIAL CRITERIA TO MONITOR OUR FINANCIAL PERFORMANCES	1	2	3	4	5	6

using an analytic technique called *factor analysis*. While the scope of this book precludes a detailed explanation of factor analytic techniques, it is important to understand the benefits it offers. Factor analysis essentially combines ratings of similar statements to produce a single evaluation of the underlying need being measured. This combination yields two benefits. First, it reduces the number of variables. As illustrated in Exhibit 10, we start with a large number of statements and end up with a substantially smaller number of combined needs measures that capture the important information in the original statement ratings. The only aspect of the original ratings discarded is inconsistency, which brings us to the second benefit of factor analysis: The combined measure of a need is more reliable than any of the separate statement ratings.

The principle here is the same as in engineering: Redundancy produces reliability. Consider a machine made of unreliable parts. If each unreliable part has enough redundant backup so that if one part fails some other part will always perform its function, then the machine as a whole can be made to be almost perfectly reliable. This is analogous to the use of factor analysis of unreliable statement ratings to produce reliable measures of needs, each formed from a combination of several statements.

Thus, it is entirely possible to identify and measure the needs motivating your business customers. Admittedly, this is a difficult process in terms of the logistics of collecting data from a multiplicity of involved decision makers, the volume of needs information required, and the analytic techniques that must be used. But it is feasible — and potentially very valuable and profitable, as we will describe in the remainder of this book.

Exhibit 10
NEEDS UNDERLYING THE STATEMENTS

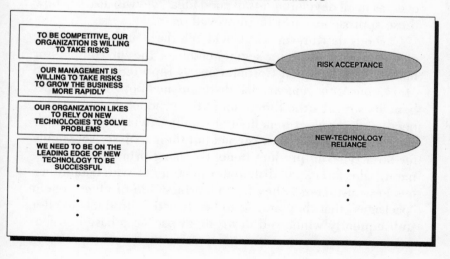

EARLIER ATTEMPTS AT NEEDS SEGMENTATION

While identifying needs in business markets is feasible, few efforts to map such needs have been reported in the marketing literature. We know of a large number of studies commissioned by private companies that will never see the light of day because of their strategic value to the companies that commissioned them. For the most part, past efforts have been focused at the level of needs for product features. As noted earlier, however, that level of need is not informative enough to provide a full understanding of fundamental customer needs affecting product choice in a complex business environment.

We have selected a few examples of business market segmentation that show early attempts at needs-based approaches. We applaud these approaches because they focus on the right things (needs) and you will get a further appreciation of the desirability of adopting a needs-based approach. However, as in all developments of good ideas, we will also see how these approaches must be improved on.

Cornelis de Kluyver and David Whitlark, at the University of Virginia, produced a segmentation of the air compressor market for Champion Corporation, as reported in *Industrial Marketing Management*, that distinguished between "product benefits sought" (the things about the product that customers need) and "product benefits deliverable" (what the marketer can produce). Thus, they carried out their analyses separately for both types of product benefits. Using primarily management, sales force, and distributor judgments (with data from a *few* key customers), they first identified 105 product benefit "packages" that they judged to be attractive products to offer (subsequently winnowed down to 43 packages based on feasibility considerations). They then collapsed SIC codes into 10 groupings they felt were attractive major industry groups. They created a matrix of industry group crossed with benefit packages and, again by judgment, designated the benefit packages to which each industry group would be attracted. Next, they arrived at 10 categories of industry groups using statistical techniques to cluster the groups according to the products they were judged to find attractive. This process was repeated for "product benefits deliverable" and eight segments were identified. The two solutions were compared in terms of their segments' relative attractiveness to Champion, and target SIC segments and appropriate product packages were selected.

As far as it goes, this is a good segmentation — a creative combination of firmographic and product-based segmentation that met Champion's short-term goals with a minimum cost. However, in common with other firmographic and product-based approaches, the approach here will not answer the *Why?* question, will not be as durable over time as we would like, is not likely to be as widely applicable across all parts of Champion Corporation, and is not very multidimensional (see Exhibit 7 in Chapter 1).

In summary, approaches such as this leave room for improvement. First and foremost, we would like to see needs analysis expanded to cover more than just product feature needs. This would make it both more durable and more widely applicable, as well as provide much deeper insight into the *Why?* question. Second, since the Champion approach uses data on SIC classes and not on individual customers, the diversity of customers that likely exists within an SIC class is not captured. Finally, judgments and evaluations directly from customers should be the primary, if not sole, basis for the segmentation. This would improve the replicability of the segmentation, as we have noted earlier.

A modification of the above approach is represented in a study of nonintelligent data terminals reported in the *Journal of Business Research* by Rowland Moriarty of Harvard and David Reibstein of Wharton. In this case, 489 individuals representing 319 DMUs rated 33 product attributes separately on "importance to you" and "difference among suppliers." Using a series of data analysis steps, these ratings were used to divide individuals into four segments: Hardware Buyers, Brand Buyers, People Buyers, and One-Stop Shoppers. The analysts then compared these benefits segments to SIC codes and number-of-employee segments and determined that, indeed, the benefits segments produced substantial differences in the product benefits sought, whereas SIC and employee size segments did not.

This approach improves on that of de Kluyver and Whitlark in that it makes direct use of customer judgments and does not rely on the opinions of those doing the selling. It uses decision makers, not SIC codes or enterprises, as the units of observation and therefore better captures the diversity of customer needs. However, it is still essentially a product-based approach and suffers from some of the same deficits: It does not fully answer the *Where?* or *Why?* questions and is weak on durability over time and on multidimensionality of coverage (see Exhibit 7 in Chapter 1). In addition, it will be most applicable to product development, but will be less useful for marketing and sales functions. Broadening the focus from only product needs to cover needs more extensively and more generally would overcome most of these deficits.

The final example of a segmentation approach is really a structure for thinking about segmentation rather than an actual segmentation application. Thomas Bonoma and Benson Shapiro at Harvard have presented a very thorough and exhaustive perspective on bases for segmentation in their book

Segmenting the Industrial Market. They describe a series of nested boxes, each containing a potential basis for segmentation (Exhibit 11).

The boxes are organized from the most easily observed and general segmentation bases on the outside to the most specific and difficult to measure on the inside. *Demographics* are the equivalent of what we refer to as firmographics. *Operating*

Exhibit 11
BONOMA AND SHAPIRO'S BOXES

Variables are stable customer characteristics focused primarily on their long-term operating, technological, and financial strengths and weaknesses. *Customer Purchasing Approaches* are DMU characteristics associated with purchasing procedures and practices, including the purely descriptive such as organization and power structures, as well as things we would recognize as needs: policies, strategies, and relationship preferences. *Situational Factors* can be thought of as transitory operating variables: They are short-term product issues, such as order fulfillment urgency, product application, or the product mix of orders. The innermost box, *Buyers' Personal Characteristics*, is comprised of internal events of individual decision makers that we would recognize as closely related to needs: motivations, perceptions, and risk management.

Bonoma and Shapiro feel that the innermost boxes represent key core elements without which the outermost elements cannot adequately account for buying differences among customers. We would certainly agree that needs are at the heart of successful segmentation, but it is not only the needs of the individual decision maker that count. A purchasing organization is not just the sum of its individual decision-making parts. Organizational or corporate needs also exist, and they reflect a corporate culture or philosophy that, to some degree, transcends individual decision makers. Certainly the individual must perform within the context of those larger corporate needs. Some of the elements described by Bonoma and Shapiro reflect corporate needs — operating variables (strengths or weaknesses) and some elements of customer purchasing approaches — but they do not appear to isolate them as such. We feel strongly that recognition should also be given to the existence and role of these larger needs.

The nested boxes offer a taxonomy of segmentation with an implied hierarchy of importance. We see many of the same elements that we have discussed previously: firmographics, situational constraints, DMU characteristics and needs (including product benefit needs), and so forth. Taxonomies are very useful for organizing, but they do not in and of themselves prescribe a course of action. In short, a taxonomy is not enough. We believe that what is lacking is a framework that describes or models customer decision making. With such a framework, a course of action for execution and implementation of a segmentation will follow and it becomes possible to organize segmentations derived from the different segmentation bases in a meaningful and useful way and to relate them to one another.

Before turning to our framework for MBS, it is worth spending a few pages on some problems that arise when marketers have attempted to use needs-based segmentation. This discussion will further lay the groundwork for some of the elements that we will incorporate into the MBS model.

PROBLEMS IN APPLYING NEEDS-BASED SEGMENTATION

The major problems with using or creating needs-based segments tend to fall into three main categories: domains of needs, types of decision makers, and reaching customers.

Domains of Needs

Medium-to-large businesses have organizational hierarchies. Their senior executives have priorities and concerns regarding a particular product category that differ from those of the functional area managers below them. Needs also differ. There are strategic needs related to factors such as price competitiveness, approach to new product development, and growth objectives. Needs associated with general business operations include needs to centrally control corporate activities for collective rather than specific goals, needs for financial controls, and needs for liquidity, or cost reduction goals. Strategic and general operations needs tend to be global and overarching in nature and, in fact, may not be fully understood by all decision makers in the DMU. Nonetheless, they shape important business purchase decisions and drive the actions of more senior managers.

At a lower level in the organization are operations needs that are specific to the product category. For example, in insurance products, the specific operations needs might be associated with purchasers' requirements for adequate coverage of their employees or with employees' needs for convenient reimbursement procedures for medical expenses. In a telephone system, specific operations needs might have to do with reliability of the system and of the service support or with end users' needs for feature functionality on the phone sets. Product-related needs fall into this category of needs.

These different domains complicate the task of attempting to understand your markets. The natural inclination when confronted with such complexity is to focus on only one of the domains, usually operations needs, specifically, product-related needs, as we have seen in previously cited studies.

Types of Decision Makers

As noted earlier, multiple decision makers and influencers usually are involved in any given product purchase decision. These individuals generally represent different functional areas or levels in the company — accounting, management, and planning, for example — in addition to the functional areas actually making the purchase and using the product. In some cases, the different functional areas involved in the decision belong to entirely different business units: Computer network decisions, for example, might be influenced by a corporate systems designer and by an end user who is actually employed by a subsidiary company. Sometimes, outsiders (third-party consultants or specifiers) are employed to help in the decision, particularly if it is a very costly or highly technical one. Architects or engineers are often hired to participate in major building or equipment decisions.

Clearly, all of these different participants are going to bring their own unique perspectives to the decision-making process. Their needs are usually subsets of the needs from the different domains outlined above, depending on the participants' functional responsibilities and managerial level.

Reaching Customers

A very common difficulty with needs-based segmentation is that of finding the customers who are members of a given segment. Remember Criterion 3 in Chapter 1 — accessibility — was one that needs-based approaches have trouble with. If all you know about a buying organization is its needs and motivations, it may be difficult to identify the best avenues for reaching its decision makers.

Furthermore, even if you know where to find customers in a given segment, it may still be difficult to decide what to say to them. Considering that different decision makers from different levels of the company are selectively concerned about different issues, how do you know what to say to any given individual to influence his or her idiosyncratic needs?

*   *   *

We will see in Chapters 3 and 4 how the diversity of needs of different decision makers can be integrated and understood within the context of a single framework. We will also discuss how to use this diversity to your advantage in marketing your products.

3

THE MARKET-DRIVEN SEGMENTATION FRAMEWORK

Through our work over the past 10 years with numerous clients in a range of industries, we have developed a highly adaptable, multidimensional framework for segmenting business markets. Designed to capture the complexity of the business environment, this market-driven framework systematically identifies the needs customers seek to satisfy when buying products and services. The framework's value in business-to-business sales lies in its applicability to a diverse range of product and service categories — as well as to mature and emerging markets in domestic and foreign environments. To demonstrate the benefits this framework offers for segmenting business markets here and abroad, this chapter describes its key features and shows you how to apply it in domestic and global markets.

SIX PRINCIPLES OF PURCHASING BEHAVIOR
IN BUSINESS MARKETS

Our segmentation framework is based on six principles that govern purchasing behavior in business markets.

1. When businesses buy products and services, multiple levels within their organizations influence the purchasing decision, either directly or indirectly.
2. During the purchasing decision process, it is likely that several levels of an organization will seek to satisfy needs that reflect their responsibilities.
3. The presence and perceived importance of a need is influenced by conditions that are external (e.g., the economy, competition, government regulations, or technology availability) and internal (e.g., finances, existing products and service commitments, or individual values).
4. While a hierarchy of needs exists within every organization, the degree of influence exerted by each level of management often depends on the perceived importance of the purchasing decision to that level's responsibilities. Strategic purchasing needs, for example, are usually considered inherently more important than operational or functional needs.
5. In any market, there are groups or segments of customers, each of which possesses a similar yet distinct configuration of needs it attempts to optimize when purchasing products and services.
6. While common needs frequently produce similar purchase behaviors within segments, differences are due to the interaction of conditions that are internal (e.g., avail-

ability of capital, the installed base, or individuals' values) and external (e.g., economic, regulatory, or technology) and that enable or constrain the realization of needs.

While a substantial body of concrete and intuitive evidence supports these principles, most business-to-business product development, marketing, and sales activities fail to factor them rigorously into their planning. Instead, there is a tendency to focus on only one "sphere of influence" within the customer organization — typically, a relevant functional buying unit, such as MIS, telecommunications, or energy management.

Evidence of this narrow approach to the business market is abundant. For example, a recent advertisement in *Business Week* by a seller of computer networking products emphasizes the ability of its software to link existing computers with future computer purchases, including different computer systems. Clearly, this ad targets computer network specialists. Despite the relatively high direct and indirect costs of installing networking software, the advertisement fails to address the needs of senior-level executives, *Business Week*'s primary audience.

Perhaps still closer to home, how many times have you heard your salespeople complain that they thought they had closed a sale, only to find out that "someone upstairs" vetoed the purchase?

Our experience in consulting assignments argues that using a framework that explicitly recognizes the six principles outlined above results in more effective product development, marketing, and sales programs. The computer network supplier, for instance, could increase its advertising effectiveness by synchronizing the advertising media with the level of buyer needs among target markets. Following this tactic, the *Business Week* advertisement would have targeted the needs of senior-level executives by promoting the long-range cost savings, reduced capital investment requirements, and improved competitive positioning that would result from lower operating overhead. A second ad placed in *Datamation* or another computer magazine could have reached computer networking specialists by emphasizing the technical features and benefits of the computer network supplier's products.

And, isn't it likely that the frustrated salespeople would have been more successful if they had covered their flank by appealing to the strategic and operation needs of senior management in addition to the needs and feature requirements of the traditional functional buyer?

Because a well-designed, insightful, and actionable segmentation is a primary contributor to strategic and tactical business success, the risk of doing it poorly demands an investment in an evaluation of all the factors with potential influence on purchasing decisions that affect your products and services.

Clearly, a successful business market segmentation must begin by identifying the major sources of purchase influence and then follow up with a systematic determination of the needs affecting the preferences of each source. Failure to recognize that the needs of several levels within the buying organization will influence the purchase decision will increase the likelihood that key differentiating factors are overlooked, and, as a consequence, the subsequent segmentation will be distorted and biased. Unfortunately, conventional approaches to business market segmentation tend to increase the likelihood of getting it wrong because they focus on the traditional buying unit and product feature preferences, ignoring the business-related needs not only of senior-level management but also of the functional buyer. The result is a misleading segmentation that fails to account for the significant influences on purchase choice.

Regardless of whether you are selling mainframe computers

or electricity, an effective business market segmentation must incorporate the six principles that govern purchasing behavior in business markets.

THE MULTIDIMENSIONAL SEGMENTATION FRAMEWORK

Now let's take a look at how a disciplined, systematic, and flexible approach can incorporate the six principles of business market purchase behavior into an effective multidimensional segmentation framework.

There is a substantial body of academic and proprietary research on the purchase decision-making process in business markets. When you sift through this research, you discover that, despite the considerable variety and complexity in formal organizational structures, there is a common infrastructure of influence. As Exhibit 12 illustrates, purchase decision making in all but the smallest businesses can be effectively reduced to three domains of influence: strategic, general business operations, and functional. Although in most businesses these domains of influence are clearly defined by formal structures and lines of authority, it is possible for them to overlap or become consolidated. Such consolidation is especially common in small businesses, where one or more individuals wear several hats and lines of authority are blurred. Nevertheless, businesses that consolidate authority must wrestle with the intrinsic influences of each level when making purchase decisions. The challenge to those who seek to segment small businesses is to recognize that multiple levels of influence exist even when there is only one formal decision maker.

Generally speaking, whether a particular level or group

plays a direct, active role in a purchasing decision depends on management style and the importance of the purchase to them. Nonetheless, it is possible that a specific management level or group can influence the outcome even if it is not directly active in the purchase decision. For instance, the prior actions of senior executives concerning purchases of a similar scope and nature can establish precedents and expectations, thereby influencing subsequent preferences or recommendations. Since it is next to impossible to determine the true influence a specific level will exert on every relevant purchase decision, the best way to avoid underestimating its potential influence is to account for it in the segmentation process.

At the peak of the organization are the senior executives (e.g., the CEO, owner, or principal) and supporting staff with responsibility for establishing the corporate mission and strategic objectives. Depending on management style and size,

Exhibit 12
TYPICAL ENTERPRISE OR BUSINESS UNIT

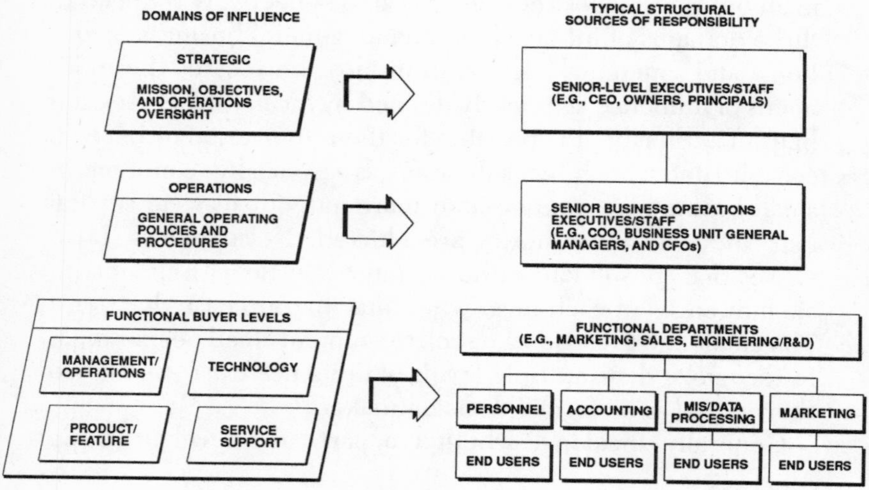

we can find a second, distinct level within the organization structure headed by the chief operating officer or business unit general manager with responsibility for planning and administering general operations policies and procedures in support of business strategic objectives.

Below the corporate or business unit level are the functional managers (e.g., finance, marketing, sales, manufacturing, MIS, telecommunications), each responsible for managing a portion of the business. At the base of the business are the end users of products and services. In most cases, we find that end users attempt to influence purchase decisions through their respective functional managers.

Product- or technology-based marketing tends to focus primarily on the requirements of the functional level of the organization. The commonly held assumption is that this middle level is the primary buyer of business-to-business products and services. Given the scope of their responsibility within the organization, it is argued that functional buyers must be a reliable source for assessing the needs of senior management, as well as the requirements of end users. Therefore, if you want to be successful, you must spend significant time and resources probing the needs of functional users.

It has been our observation that most business-to-business sellers base their product development, marketing, sales, and service strategies and tactics almost exclusively on the feedback from this midlevel functional category of so-called buyers. While it is obvious that middle management is a legitimate target, focusing exclusively on this level frequently produces a mutually reinforcing form of technology- or product-focused tunnel vision. The trap is caused by a mutual affinity between seller and buyer around the product, its features, and direct benefits. This affinity results in a skewed and often misleading inadequacy of representation of the needs of other management levels within the organization.

Categories of Need

Although our approach recognizes that the functional buyer is a prime target, it argues that technology- and feature-based myopia can be avoided only by explicitly identifying the needs of all significant domains of influence affecting the purchase. Once captured, this comprehensive needs profile serves as the foundation for a segmentation program that can be used to effectively guide product development, marketing, and sales. When domains of influence are mapped against categories of need, the potential value of this approach becomes clear. Exhibit 13 illustrates this mapping.

Strategic Needs

In our framework, business strategy needs such as access to capital, growth through competitive pricing, or superior service are conditioned by external, environmental factors such as the state of the economy, government regulations, and discrete competitive challenges. Generally speaking, strategic needs are formulated by senior executives at the corporate or business unit level and explicitly or implicitly guide most purchase decisions made by subordinates in the organization.

Failure to account for these strategic needs in the segmentation can significantly limit the effectiveness of the market planning and in the end produce higher selling costs. For example, if the computer network supplier had really understood the differential strategic needs of its market, then the message in its *Business Week* advertisement would have focused on the strategic needs of its target markets.

In addition to enhancing marketing and sales effectiveness, incorporating strategic needs into the segmentation can improve the effectiveness of product development efforts. For instance, IBM walked away from an enormous opportunity as it migrated from the PC to the PS/2. The PS/2 product ignored affordability in favor of functionality and high margins. As a result, IBM conceded a substantial portion of the home, small business, and even corporate market to PC-clone manufacturers. If IBM had fully appreciated the significance of price or

Exhibit 13
DOMAINS OF INFLUENCE MAPPED TO CATEGORIES OF NEED

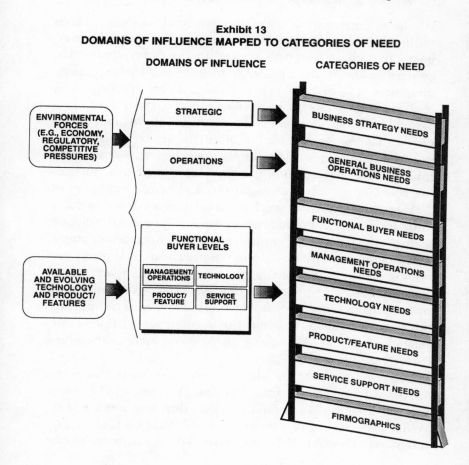

affordability as a driver of purchase, it might have modified its product development and pricing strategy to capitalize on the opportunity.

General Business Operations Needs

We have interviewed many thousands of medium-to-large businesses over the last several years, and virtually every business we have talked to has a general set of administrative policies and procedures designed to guide day-to-day management in a manner that is theoretically, if not actually, consistent with its strategic objectives. In the context of these general operations policies and procedures, there exists a set of needs that the business attempts to satisfy when acquiring products and services. Generally speaking, these needs fall into five categories: planning, organization structure, purchasing rules, cost-control mechanisms, and management styles.

A segmentation framework that explicitly accounts for differentiation among operations needs can help product developers scale products to satisfy centralized or decentralized organizational requirements and design administrative support and pricing packages that satisfy planning horizon, organizational structure, and cost-management needs. Marketing can benefit by leveraging knowledge about these needs into competitive positioning strategies, while the recognition of operations-related needs can help sales anticipate and manage its selling cycle.

Classic examples of the failure to recognize operations needs are often found in the area of billing. For years, AT&T sent separate monthly bills for each long-distance service (e.g., WATS, 800 service, private lines) to each location of an organization. As a consequence, businesses with many locations that had centralized accounts payable were forced to spend considerable effort each month consolidating these bills. MCI and US Sprint discovered this need, developed a consolidated billing product, and used the product as a marketing vehicle to gain a more favorable competitive position against AT&T.

Functional Buyer Needs

With the exception of small companies, every organization tends to divide management of its business into functional areas at some level. Depending on the products or services sold, at least one of these functional units is likely to be the traditional target buyer. For example, if you sell telecommunications products and services, the target functional buyer is usually telecommunications or network management. Since this individual or group is the primary pre- and postsale contact, it is essential to carefully identify and catalog its needs.

We have uncovered three common flaws in the ways in which most companies analyze and diagnose the needs of their primary target buyers. First, there is a tendency to focus almost exclusively on the technical or product feature related characteristics these buyers seek, while ignoring the underlying reasons for interest in those technology or product features. For instance, major telecommunications equipment and service providers spend considerable money and effort to identify customer data communications bandwidth or transmission speed requirements. This approach ignores the underlying reasons for bandwidth — namely cost savings, faster throughput and response times, and enhanced applications capability.

The second flaw we have observed is the failure to systematically catalog the full set of requirements needed by the functional target group. The common approach is to construct a laundry list of "needs" that mixes technology, features, functionality, vendor support, and operations management requirements. There are two drawbacks to this approach. First, it tends to produce an incomplete list of needs, and, second, it fails to rank categories of need by target group (e.g., are operations management needs actually more important than technology or feature needs?). A more systematic approach first identifies the categories of need (e.g., technology, product category features and functionality, vendor service support, and operations management) and then specifies customer requirements and the reasons behind them within each category. This approach produces a richer understanding of the needs associated with specific product characteristics, as well as the relative importance of the categories of need. But even more important, use of this approach promotes the design of strategies and tactics that customers will truly perceive as *distinct* — strategies and tactics that are not just a veneer superficially designed to distinguish vendors but that do not actually move buyers.

The third flaw in conventional methods used to diagnose the needs of target functional buyers is a tendency to collect information only from the largest customers. Generally we hear two rationales for this approach. The first is the contention that these large customers generate the most money. The second, more tenuous claim is that large customers represent the leading edge of the market. Given lengthy product development cycles, if products are developed for the whole market based on the needs of market leaders, then by the time those products reach the market, there is a high probability that they will fit the needs of the large mass of followers. According to this rationale, focusing on the needs of market leaders can have a valuable "trickle-down" impact on mass market sales.

Clearly, the needs of large customers must be identified; however, using the needs of large customers as the sole basis for product development ignores the fact that the great mass of buyers may never possess the scale and scope of technology needs demanded by larger customers, let alone the ability to afford their satisfaction. A more effective strategy is not to assume a common set of technology needs across all customers, but rather to systematically identify the special needs of representative groups of potential customers.

In summary, our approach to the needs of the functional target group is to identify categories of needs and then to systematically identify within each category the specific requirements of a representative sample of customers. For example, we have found that the telecommunications functional target possesses four broad categories of needs: operations management, technology, product category, and vendor support. Within each of these categories there are specific needs that differentiate customer groups.

Firmographics

While the primary tool for segmenting customers within our framework is needs-based analysis, we have discovered that needs alone do not predict a product preference or choice. In some cases, customers who share common needs purchase different products. The explanation for this phenomenon is quite simple. Factors such as available capital, the installed base of products, or industry type can place constraints on the options available to some customers, and, as a consequence, these customers are forced to make choices that do not fully satisfy their needs.

Our framework accounts for the presence and relative effect

of these firmographic factors in two steps. First, the research effort supporting the segmentation is designed to identify and measure fixed and temporary factors including environmental influences. Each segment is then profiled using these descriptive characteristics. These profiles allow you to identify relevant differences in firmographics across and within segments. The second step involves an analysis of the relationship between firmographic characteristics, needs, and product choices for each customer studied. These analyses allow you to assess the relationship of temporary and fixed factors to needs, as well as the relationship of needs and firmographic factors to product choice.

Variations in the Influence of Needs Dimensions

All needs are not created equal. In general, strategic and general business operations needs have more potential influence on product and service decisions than the needs of functional buyers because they are more critical to an organization's success. Clearly, the extent to which strategic or operations needs directly influence any specific product choice will depend on several factors, including the perceived relevance of the decision to the strategic position, general operating policies and procedures of the organization, as well as the purchase situation. For example, in cases for which the purchase involves a significant capital outlay, such as the purchase of a large computer, strategic and operations needs are likely to influence the decision directly. Conversely, when the decision involves relatively small amounts of money, strategic and operations needs are likely to have less direct influence on the decision; however, even in these rather low-risk situations, strategic and operations needs may implicitly affect the choice, establishing boundaries within which the choice must be made.

The purchase situation also affects the degree to which strategic and operations needs influence the purchase decision. For instance, functional-level needs may have more influence on the purchase when the decision is a simple rebuy or replace decision or when narrowly defined technical needs are satisfied by the purchase without any strategic or operational implications. When Mobil Oil purchases fuel additives that satisfy narrowly defined specifications, the role strategic and operations needs play is secondary to the influence of functional needs. However, when the purchase decision also involves a change in the formula or mix of additives to reduce carbon buildup in automobile fuel-injection systems, we can expect strategic and operations needs to exert influence because the choice will affect Mobil's strategic position in the marketplace.

Applications and Benefits of the Framework

A brief snapshot of the output from this segmentation framework will help you appreciate both the richness and benefits of the information the framework can produce and the applications it can support. As a note, in the next chapter, we describe alternative methods for gathering and analyzing data that will populate the framework while Chapters 5 and 6 discuss strategic and tactical applications of the information.

Potential Information Outputs

At the most rudimentary level, the framework is a vehicle for organizing and summarizing information provided by representatives of your markets. The information you get will be a function of what you solicit from the market. However, the framework can produce the following information for the market as a whole and for segments in particular:

1. a prioritized list of relevant needs organized by their source: strategy, operations, and functional buyer
2. appropriate descriptive information (e.g., industry type, size, expenditures, installed base competitive share)
3. preferences for distribution and sales channels, product features, pricing, new products
4. future purchase intentions including preferred vendor, number of units, and expected timing of purchase
5. customer trade-offs of one product feature for another, for use in estimating the demand, revenues, and share potential of alternative product packages
6. specification of the decision-making process, including roles and relative influence

THE SEGMENTATION AS MEANS OF STRUCTURING MARKET INFORMATION

Once you have collected information from the market in the context of this framework, the next step is a division of the market into segments representing unique patterns of needs. These segments can be described by their firmographic characteristics and other relevant information such as their decision-making tendencies, channel preferences, or future purchase intentions. Exhibit 14 illustrates the form of the segments.

Focusing on two segments, Exhibit 15 demonstrates that the segmentation output will highlight differences in the direction and intensity of needs within and across the segments. Note, for instance, the subtle yet important differences between Segments 1 and 4 in the intensity and direction of expressed strategic needs. Both segments express a similar inclination to

Exhibit 14
RELATIVE DISTRIBUTION OF DOMAINS OF NEED
ACROSS SEGMENTS

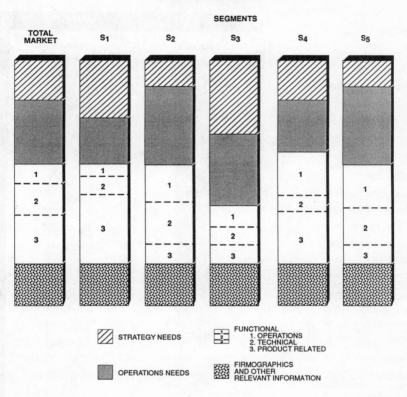

take risks and adopt new technologies, yet the motivations for early adoption are quite different. In the case of Segment 1, needs to take risks to grow and adopt new technology appear to be driven by the pressures of competitive pricing and market expansion. In contrast, risk and new technology adoption appear to be motivated in Segment 4 by efforts to expand markets

Exhibit 15
EXAMPLE OF INTENSITY AND DIRECTION OF NEEDS
WITHIN SEGMENTS

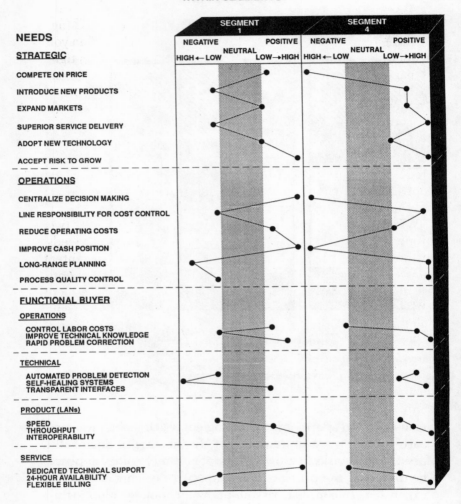

and differentiate on superior service and new product introductions.

At the general business operations level, the differences are not so subtle. Segment 1 wants centralized decision making, operating expense reduction, and more capital. The vision you get of this segment is of hierarchical operation focused on tight management of financials — a vision that is not inconsistent with its expressed strategic need to compete on price.

Customers in Segment 4 are quite different. Consistent with their strategic objective of differentiating themselves by providing superior service, these customers seek to improve quality control at operations level. This need is complemented by long-range planning and line-management empowerment to control costs. Access to capital in order to address these needs does not appear to be a problem.

When we move down to the functional buyer level, two properties of the segmentation are apparent. First, the needs expressed here are closer to the traditional product-oriented view of the market. And second, members of the segments are motivated by different operations, technical, product, and service needs. Customers in Segment 4 want fast, efficient, and user-transparent communications systems that proactively detect and automatically correct problems before they affect the user or the customer. In addition, they want the suppliers to be there when they need them and provide flexible billing.

Members of Segment 1 also want rapid problem detection, as well as a responsive system whose operating differences are transparent to the user. However, these customers apparently want to lean more heavily on the vendors for technical support as a means of reducing labor costs.

With these snapshots in mind, how would you apply this information to build strategy and tactics?

APPLICATIONS OVERVIEW

When wrapped in this segmentation framework, market information becomes an extremely valuable strategic and tactical weapon. At the strategic level, the segmentation provides you with a fundamental starting point for understanding the structure of your markets. Among the important structure questions you will want to answer are: How big is the market? What is our share of the market? Who are our customers? How are our customers different than those of our competitors? What needs are motivating the market? How big are the segments? How are we doing in each? In which segments are we advantaged and how? Where are we at risk and why?

Once you understand the structure of the market, you can use the segmentation to help you select and target markets. Some of the key selection and targeting issues you will want to investigate include: What is the revenue opportunity offered by each segment? What is the profitability potential? How do our capabilities, e.g., product portfolio, service support, development resources, technical expertise, manufacturing, and delivery, compare with the needs of the segments? How is the competition likely to measure up?

Product developers can compare the segment needs with needs that existing or planned products satisfy to identify gaps in the product line or uncover opportunities for new products. If product concept evaluations or product feature trade-off exercises are included in the segmentation data collection effort, then product development will get explicit direction about new product opportunities or product feature and price optimization by segment.

Marketing and sales can use the segmentation to define the appropriate marketing mix for the target segments. The needs can be used to shape positioning strategies, sales pitches, and advertising messages. Information about segment-level distribution and sales channel preferences can be used to define and support channel strategies and tactics.

Finally, it is possible to use the segmentation information to develop tools that will enable sales to assign customers to segments prior to a direct contact. For instance, we have used easily accessible firmographic information from suppliers like Dun & Bradstreet to assign customers preliminarily to segments. While we describe how this link is accomplished in Chapter 4, it is important to point out that the ability to prequalify customers into segments gives sales a valuable prospecting tool that can improve the hit rate on sales efforts.

The Benefits

The MBS framework has three general attributes. First, the concept of segmenting customers on categories of needs such as strategy, operations, and functional buyer is intuitively sensible. Second, the framework seems to capture reasonably the "reality" of a complex business market. And third, the framework possesses an attractive simplicity in its organization of needs into domains.

On closer inspection, the framework offers concrete business benefits:

- ability to continuously differentiate your products and services on a basis that is meaningful to the customer — the customer's needs
- improved competitive positioning, market share, revenues, and profitability by understanding, and responding to, the motivators of purchase (needs) in segments offering

attractive revenue opportunities and higher potential rates of return
- ability to get out in front of the competition by quickly capitalizing on new product opportunities associated with unmet needs
- ability to stay in front of the competition by routinely tracking segment performance, product requirements, needs, and sizes
- improved new product success rates by shaping products, product portfolios, and product packages and pricing to fit the needs of target segments
- realized economies of scale in marketing and selling by defining product portfolios targeted to segments offering high revenue and profitability potential
- saved money through more precise market planning and improved coordination of product development, marketing sales, and strategy
- increased efficiency and effectiveness of selling efforts by prequalifying customers on segment membership and tailoring selling messages to fit segment and purchase influencer needs
- obtained economies and improved returns from distribution channels choices

One caveat is necessary. Realization of these and other benefits will depend on whether you use the tools effectively.

THE FRAMEWORK IN ACTION

To help you better understand the value of the framework in the context of your markets, we need to impose reality on what has been a theoretical discussion to this point. In the example below, we describe an actual application of the framework to segment the business market for electric utility services.

The Electric Utility Market

In response to the energy crisis, Three Mile Island, and dramatic increases in the capital costs of generating electricity, the electric utility industry developed a demand-side strategy aimed at motivating customers to manage their energy consumption. To make the demand-side strategy work, an industry focused on the supply side had to climb the marketing learning curve quickly. In the early 1980s, the Electric Power Research Institute (EPRI) was instructed by its utility membership to develop and disseminate state-of-the-art marketing and research tools. Toward this end, EPRI initiated the Customer Preference and Behavior Project (CP&B) in 1985. Between 1985 and 1988, the CP&B project concentrated on the residential market, producing a residential energy market segmentation framework (CLASSIFY℠) and a new product development model (PULSE℠) supported by training materials designed to "transfer know-how" to marketing and research personnel within individual utilities. In 1988, a similar effort was initiated by EPRI for the business market. The results of this extensive research effort serve as the basis of this example.

The Market

Electric utilities have developed a variety of programs and services to encourage business customers to adopt energy management behaviors. Some of these programs require the installation of energy-efficient equipment, such as lighting, heating, ventilation and air-conditioning (HVAC), or refrigeration, while other programs involve incentives to modify consumption behaviors, such as time-of-day rates to stimulate shifts in energy usage from peak to off-peak use. The customer investments and savings associated with participation in these programs can range dramatically, from several hundred dollars to millions, depending on the program and size of the customer.

The primary target for these programs and services is usually an individual, or group of individuals, with responsibility for managing energy; however, senior-level management may be involved directly or indirectly in the decision. In addition, the decision can be made either at the local site or by corporate headquarters.

Categories of Needs

The definition of the categories of needs, as well as the needs within levels, required four iterative stages of market research. In the first stage, a series of in-depth interviews were conducted with 30 businesses, across the United States, that had recently made a decision to participate or not participate in a utility-sponsored demand-side management program. Exploration of their decision processes revealed three common influences. These included (1) senior-level executives, whose participation focused on the satisfaction of needs related to business strategy; (2) executives and staff who were concerned about what kind of impact participation in the program would have on general business operations; and (3) those responsible for managing energy services and operations, who attempted to satisfy needs related to power delivery and service.

Following these interviews, focus groups were used to build a list of needs within each category. Next, two iterations of pilot surveys were conducted to filter and refine the needs within each category. Armed with a set of needs within each category and a thoroughly tested set of questions designed to measure these needs, a national survey was completed using a representative sample of commercial establishments throughout the United States. The national survey produced four general dimensions of needs: business strategy, general business operations, energy operations, and end-use-specific needs.

Exhibit 16 identifies the needs in each dimension. End uses (e.g., cooling, heating, lighting) are analogous to product categories. For the purposes of segmentation, the needs for each end use are treated separately. Such a treatment results in the ability to segment the overall market using only needs related

Exhibit 16
ENERGY RELATED NEEDS DIMENSIONS

BUSINESS STRATEGY
• MARKET NEW PRODUCTS/SERVICES
• LEAD THROUGH NEW TECHNOLOGY ADOPTION
• TAKE RISKS TO GROW BUSINESS
• COMPETE ON PRICE
• PROVIDE SUPERIOR SERVICE
• EMPHASIZE QUALITY OVER SHORT-TERM COSTS

GENERAL BUSINESS OPERATIONS
• FOCUS ON LONG-RANGE MANAGEMENT
• CENTRALIZED DECISION MAKING
• LINE RESPONSIBILITY FOR COST CONTROL
• IMPROVE CASH POSITION
• USE NEW TECHNOLOGY TO IMPROVE OPERATIONS
• LEASE EQUIPMENT

ENERGY OPERATIONS NEEDS
• INVEST IN ENERGY SAVING TECHNIQUES
• MANAGE ENERGY USE
• MAXIMIZE EQUIPMENT EFFICIENCY
• BACKUP GENERATION
• CLEAN POWER
• CONTINUOUS POWER
• RATE STABILITY
• FLEXIBLE BILLING
• CUSTOMIZED SERVICE
• SUPPORTIVE UTILITY RELATIONSHIPS

END-USE NEEDS
LIGHTING NEEDS

SPACE COOLING NEEDS
• PROTECT PRODUCTS AND EQUIPMENT
• MAINTAIN EMPLOYEE COMFORT
• ACQUIRE RELIABLE EQUIPMENT
• REDUCE OPERATING COSTS
• REDUCE INITIAL COSTS
• PROVIDE MODULAR TEMPERATURE CONTROLS

71

Exhibit 17
ENERGY NEEDS SEGMENTATION STRUCTURE

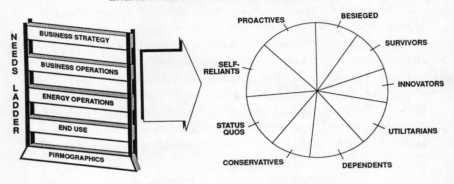

to strategy, operations, and target functions. Beyond this more general market segmentation, it is then possible to segment markets within product categories based on end uses.

The Segments

Analysis of the national survey produced nine needs-based segments within the business energy market. Each segment has a unique pattern of needs.

The segment labels in Exhibit 17 are merely convenient reminders chosen to assist the user in recalling each segment's pattern of needs. After all, the needs that customers attempt to satisfy when they consider participation in a utility-sponsored demand-side program are most important. Exhibit 18 provides a brief profile of needs for each segment.

Given this context, how can electric utilities use our segmentation framework and data to design marketing strategies, shape program offerings, and implement effective sales and promotion efforts?

Exhibit 18
NEEDS PROFILES OF SEGMENTS

PROACTIVES: Actively managed centralized price competitors, who adopt new technologies, supervise energy use, and seek supportive utility relationships

BESIEGED: Day-to-day managers with low energy costs, who are driven largely by near-term cash concerns

SURVIVORS: Investors in new technologies, who strive to improve cash flow by competing on price and learning equipment

INNOVATORS: Risk-taking leaders in quality, who develop new products and services, embrace new technologies, and require clean and continuous power

UTILITARIANS: Multilocational businesses, who manage for the long term, prefer to lease equipment, and seek to provide new and superior services

DEPENDENTS: Energy managers, who require uninterrupted power, want customized services, and need flexibility in billing

CONSERVATIVES: Service-oriented, centralized cost controllers, who seek clean power, rate stability, and supportive utility relationships

STATUS QUOS: Confident managers of mature product lines, who have low-percentage energy costs

SELF-RELIANTS: Quality-oriented, day-to-day line managers, whose businesses do not depend heavily on energy supply or services

Designing Marketing Strategies

For a utility seeking to manage electric service usage, the primary strategic objective is to produce optimal reductions in electric demand during peak hours without losing customers to the competition — gas suppliers or self-generation, for instance. What insights does the needs-based segmentation offer utility marketing strategists?

Even a cursory review of the needs profiles in Exhibit 18 makes it evident that a generic marketing strategy would be suboptimal. Adopting a positioning based solely on reduced cost or incentives to transfer some usage to off-peak or acquire energy-efficient equipment will appeal to segments expressing a need to remain cost competitive or to control operating costs. These needs are prevalent among only three of the nine segments: Proactives, Survivors, and Conservatives. Alternatively, a position focused on social responsibility for conserving valuable energy resources will also have a limited reach, appealing to two who value utility relationships and will be responsive to cost savings: Proactives and Conservatives.

Based upon the needs of the segments, it would appear that an optimal marketing strategy would require a diversified, rather than a generic, positioning to an initial subset of segments. Due to low interest in and low usage of electricity, utilities would be advised to identify and exclude customers who are members of the Besieged, Status Quo, and Self-Reliant segments (techniques for assigning customers to segments will be discussed in subsequent chapters). Among the remaining segments, low cost and social responsibility positions are likely to appeal to Proactives, Survivors, and Conservatives. Positionings focused on improving the efficiency and reliability of electric equipment are likely to strike a responsive chord among Innovators, Utilitarians, and Dependents by appealing to their need for continuous, clean power and superior service delivery to their own customers.

Once marketing strategies are defined, electric utilities can use the segmentation as a guide for identifying product opportunities, prioritizing program development activities, and targeting programs. To demonstrate how the segmentation can be used in this manner, let us take a look at two target segments: Proactives and Dependents.

Product Development and Program Prioritization and Targeting

The energy operations needs of Proactives and Dependents provide program and service developers in the utility industry with insight into new product and service program opportunities, as well as direction on the general characteristics programs will have to possess to be received favorably by each of these segments. For example, a close examination of Exhibit 19 reveals new service opportunities. Both segments express a rather strong need for flexible billing. More specifically, members of these segments want more detailed energy usage information. To satisfy this need, utilities can develop management-reporting summaries that include breakdowns of current and historical usage by location to help customers in these two segments better manage and control energy consumption. As well as flexible billing, both segments report a need for backup generation. Obviously, the utility could sell backup generators to these segments. Other opportunities for the segments may be identified by further examination of the profiles.

Exhibit 19
SEGMENT PROFILES

	PROACTIVES	DEPENDENTS
NEEDS	RELATIVE STRENGTH OF NEED	RELATIVE STRENGTH OF NEED
	LOW NEUTRAL HIGH	LOW NEUTRAL HIGH

BUSINESS STRATEGY
- TAKE RISKS TO GROW BUSINESS
- PROVIDE SUPERIOR SERVICE
- MARKET NEW PRODUCTS/SERVICES
- EMPHASIZE QUALITY OVER SHORT-TERM COSTS
- LEAD THROUGH NEW TECHNOLOGY ADOPTION
- COMPETE ON PRICE

BUSINESS OPERATIONS
- USE NEW TECHNOLOGY TO IMPROVE OPERATIONS
- IMPROVED CASH POSITION
- FOCUS ON LONG-RANGE MANAGEMENT
- LEASING EQUIPMENT
- CENTRALIZED DECISION MAKING
- LINE RESPONSIBILITY FOR COST CONTROL

ENERGY OPERATIONS
- SUPPORTIVE UTILITY RELATIONSHIPS
- INVEST IN ENERGY-SAVING TECHNOLOGIES
- BACKUP GENERATION
- MANAGE ENERGY USE
- CLEAN POWER
- FLEXIBLE BILLING
- CUSTOMIZED SERVICE
- RATE STABILITY
- CONTINUOUS POWER
- MAXIMIZE EQUIPMENT EFFICIENCY

FIRMOGRAPHICS	%	%
BUSINESS CHARACTERISTICS		
SINGLE LOCATION COMPANY	21	48
MORE THAN 20 FULL-TIME EMPLOYEES	63	70
NONFOOD RETAIL/WHOLESALE ESTABLISHMENTS	26	25
BUILDING SPACE CHARACTERISTICS		
LOW-RISE OFFICE BUILDING	29	27
100,000 OR MORE SQUARE FEET	7	14
ENERGY CHARACTERISTICS		
ENERGY COSTS 10% OR MORE OF OPERATING BUDGET	36	26
COGENERATION CONSIDERED OR INSTALLED IN LAST THREE YEARS	16	10
OVERALL LOAD IMPACT	HIGH	MODERATE

J-F

In the case of the EPRI research, the national survey offered demand-side program designers additional guidance. The survey presented several demand-side program concepts to customers and asked them to indicate a likelihood of participation in each. As Exhibit 20 illustrates, the propensity to participate in these programs varied by segment. Although utilities are counseled to make program selections on the basis of the relationship between potential consumption affected and likely acceptance across all segments, it is clear that Proactives are attracted to heat pump, cool storage, air conditioner maintenance, time-of-use (TOU) rates, and heat recovery programs while Dependents are likely to participate in efficient lighting and air conditioner maintenance programs.

The needs expressed by these segments provide insight about the differential appeal of programs as well as why particular programs are attractive to each segment. The heat pump, cool storage, air conditioner maintenance, TOU rates, and heat recovery programs are attractive to Proactives because the incentives, rebates, and reduced energy costs promised by these programs appeal to the Proactives' need to reduce operating expenses as a way to achieve price competitiveness. In

Exhibit 20
PROGRAM PARTICIPATION PROPENSITY BY SEGMENT

PROGRAMS	PROACTIVES	DEPENDENTS
• HEAT PUMP	●	○
• EFFICIENT LIGHTING	○	●
• COOL STORAGE	●	○
• AIR CONDITIONER MAINTENANCE	●	●
• INTERRUPTIBLE LOAD	○	○
• TOU RATES	●	○
• HEAT RECOVERY	●	○

● HIGH
○ LOW

addition, these programs appeal to several energy operations needs reported by Proactives, namely, the need to manage energy use, stabilize rates, maximize equipment efficiency, and develop a mutually supportive relationship with their utilities.

Dependents react favorably to efficient lighting and air conditioner maintenance programs because they appeal not only to energy operations needs to invest in energy-saving technologies and manage energy use, but they do so without jeopardizing the strategic need to deliver superior service.

Sales and Promotion

Suppose a utility decided to sell and promote an air conditioner maintenance program. Proactives and Dependents would be target markets. In promoting such a program, marketing could use a common message for both segments. Such a positioning would focus on long-term operating cost savings, maximization of operating equipment efficiencies, and the ability to better control energy costs. The major difference between the segments is the preferred distribution channel for the program. Proactives would be more likely to participate in the program if they had a choice among maintenance suppliers. In contrast, Dependents would prefer maintenance to be handled by the utility.

The segmentation firmographics indicate that field sales personnel are most likely to find Proactives and Dependents in large, multilocation retail and wholesale establishments (see Exhibit 19). Moreover, because the required annual investment is less than $10,000, energy operations functionaries are likely to be solely responsible for the decision to participate. Therefore, a single-tier sell is required, and the decision cycle is likely to be short.

USING THE MBS FRAMEWORK
IN FOREIGN MARKETS

Up to this point, we have confined our discussion to applications of the segmentation framework in U.S. markets. However, our multinational consulting experience suggests that the six principles of business decision making that serve as the foundation of the framework apply in virtually every national or regional market. Consequently, it can be used for segmenting markets in countries other than the United States. Moreover, the framework is flexible enough to accommodate cross-national segmentation in support of global product development, marketing, and sales activities.

The MBS Framework in Europe and Japan

As we write this chapter, we are engaged in applying the framework in Europe and Japan. Preliminary research indicates the presence of similar categories of needs to those we have found in the United States. While we have yet to conclude our research and analysis, we expect significant similarities across nations in strategic, general business operations, and target function needs. Nonetheless, some national and regional variations are expected.

In Europe, for example, the impending economic integration under the EEC in 1992 is likely to produce a strong perceived strategic need for Pan-European competitive differentiation. However, most of the variation among countries is expected to be confined to differences in direction and intensity around a similar set of needs within each category. For instance, we expect that "centralized decision making" will be more prevalent and more intensely expressed by Japanese companies than by U.S. companies.

Despite the existence of some cross-national differences, we expect that several segments discovered in one country will exist in other countries, but the numbers of customers in the segments are likely to differ from country to country. Confirmation of this finding will have significant implications for global applications of the framework.

The Growing Need for a Global Segmentation

With the growing momentum toward globalization of markets and products, businesses selling in international markets will need a single segmentation framework flexible enough to capture similarities across, and differences within, nations. Such a segmentation framework can create considerable efficiencies for product development, marketing, and sales in a global environment. For instance, a common framework would help product developers identify and size segments with common feature requirements and thus support investment planning. These commonalities could be used to design core product lines with cross-national appeal. Extensions to core products can be developed to account for differences within countries.

Similar efficiencies can accrue to marketing and sales. For instance, the ability to identify the presence of cross-national segments with common patterns of needs permits marketers to develop efficient and effective cross-national targeting and positioning strategies. At the same time, sensitivity to national differences in needs will support the identification of subtle within-nation differences for country-specific marketing activities. National and global sales forces can use segmentation data to more efficiently locate prospects and customize selling activities to reflect more effectively the complex structure of customer needs.

The characteristics of the multidimensional framework make it a primary candidate for use in multinational or global segmentation efforts. In the first place, the framework is constructed on principles of business decision making that cut across national and cultural boundaries. Second, the framework is sufficiently flexible to account for national differences. Finally, the framework will reveal similar patterns of need across multinational markets.

SUMMARY

As you confront the challenges of growing your business in the 1990s, your chances of success can be improved by recognizing and responding to the changing needs of your markets. To help you in this endeavor, we have described a framework that our research indicates can provide you with significant advantages regardless of the products and services you sell or the countries within which you sell.

Among the most important advantages the framework offers is its focus on the needs customers seek to satisfy when they acquire your products and services. By concentrating on customer needs, the framework forces you to become more market than technology or product driven. Such a market orientation will help you keep your current customers happy and beat your competition to market with products and services that meet emerging needs.

Of equal importance is the recognition that customer needs are not confined to product features and functions but are multidimensional, reflecting the dynamic environment in which products and services are bought and used. By capturing the multidimensionality of needs, the framework helps you not only improve product development, but also create more effective competitive market positioning for your products and services.

Additionally, the framework can help you improve the efficiency and effectiveness of your sales force. Like other forms of segmentation, the framework can not only help your sales force characterize prospects once they have met them, but also target potential buyers in advance of a direct contact; however, unlike other segmentation techniques, this framework provides your sales force with information about where the likely targets are, what levels within the buying organization are likely to be critical sources of influence on a purchase decision, as well as what needs each influencer on the purchase is seeking to satisfy through the purchase. This information can be used to improve the effectiveness of advertising, promotions, and sales activities.

Finally, the framework is sufficiently comprehensive to support a lasting, dynamic market-driven program in a national or international market. In the remaining chapters, we show you how to create a market-driven business segmentation and how to use it.

4

CREATING A
NEEDS-BASED
SEGMENTATION

The construction of the segmentation is likely to be one of the most significant and "living" investments your business will make. It is significant because the insight you gain from the segmentation will continually feed and verify strategic decisions such as how to truly differentiate your products and services, what the critical success factors are that the market thinks are important, or how to position or reposition products and services.

Like a good investment, its value appreciates rather than depreciates over time. You can realize relatively quick returns by selecting and targeting your marketing, product development, and sales efforts toward compatible high-yield segments. At the street level, the ability to prequalify customers and arm salespeople with trigger messages can improve sales hit rates.

In addition, the investment will yield long-term appreciation because it has "living" properties. Once you have built the segmentation platform, you will be able to cost effectively leverage the benchmark framework to track changes in the size and shape of segments semiannually or annually. Moreover, you can monitor segment membership of buyers over time and fine-tune your strategy, product development, marketing, and sales efforts to produce even more efficient and effective returns on your investment.

In this chapter, we discuss the nuts and bolts of developing the framework and the data to support an MBS approach to your markets. Recognizing that the resources to invest in this form of segmentation will vary, we divide the chapter into two sections. The first section describes the Deep Approach — the method that yields the richest return with the lowest risk. The second section describes two Budget Approaches that do not provide the depth or statistical confidence of the preferred approach; however, they can produce some of the basic tools to get you started.

GETTING STARTED

Regardless of approach, once you have decided to segment your markets using the MBS-based framework, we have found it is imperative to form an internal working team composed of three broad user groups: marketing, product management, and sales. Active involvement of each of these user groups in the segmentation process builds understanding of and comfort with the infrastructure and potential applications of the framework while creating a shared sense of ownership. We find that clients who invest in establishing common understanding and ownership among these crucial parties avoid subsequent criticism that the segmentation is not useful. But even more important, when the segmentation is completed, team members become champions of the approach within their respective divisions. As a consequence, the business tends to get maximum value from the segmentation because implementation is coordinated and comprehensive.

One final word of start-up advice: Be certain to take time to educate relevant senior-level executives about the segmentation framework, its applications, and its expected benefits. It has been our experience that this investment will produce the support you need to get the most out of the segmentation effort for your organization.

THE OBJECTIVES

Our needs-based segmentation approach requires considerable discipline without which you risk, among other things, generating an unstructured laundry list of market-related phenomena that might or might not include some needs. More often than not, this list will include a large number of descriptive properties of products or features. While some of these may be useful, they dilute the real focus, which is the identification of needs — the internal motivations, such as product preference and vendor choice, that drive market behaviors. Discipline begins with a clear specification of objectives for gathering market-based information. While we cannot definitively account for the specific objectives every organization might seek to satisfy, we can offer some guidance.

Since the entire segmentation sits on a foundation of needs, a first-order objective must be the development of a comprehensive and accurate list of the needs. These needs must reflect motivations that are internal to customers who are representative of current and potential markets. The needs must be important to the customer, and they must have a future orientation; that is, they may be felt now and are expected to be present in the near future, or they are on the radar scope for the future. Finally, the needs of all domains of influence on the purchase of the product categories you sell must be identified.

The second broad objective of information gathering is to collect data that will permit you to reliably project the size of subsequent segments. These data may include numbers of companies, counts of the installed base of relevant products, or units of service usage. Where possible, it is useful to obtain near-term estimates of growth, for example, the number of replacements or new purchases that can be expected in the next two to three years.

A third objective is to collect sufficient descriptive firm-ographic and product-usage data so that you can anchor the segments in a reality that sales and product development will find credible and useful.

Once you are internally organized and your objectives are defined, you are ready to go find out what the market needs.

THE DEEP APPROACH

The Deep Approach involves two comprehensive phases of research. In the first phase, rigorous qualitative research is conducted to identify and refine needs. The methods used include fairly structured in-depth, in-person interviews or focus groups with representatives of the domains of influence — senior executives and business unit managers, as well as key influentials in the relevant functional buying unit. To avoid missing pockets of needs, you must be certain to include a mix of organizations that represents your market.

The second phase requires a survey across a larger representative sample of organizations and establishments within the market of interest. The primary objectives of the survey are to identify needs-based segments, estimate the size of the segments, and profile the nonneeds characteristics of the segments (e.g., industry membership). The survey is an opportunity to capture other important information about the segments, including distribution and channel preferences, reactions to new product concepts, feature package preferences, and decision-making practices.

The Deep Approach offers significant advantages over the Budget Approaches. First, by casting the net wide and deep, you substantially reduce the likelihood of missing important and evolving needs. Second, robust and representative quantitative research provides greater statistical confidence in the segmentation itself. In other words, the segmentation is likely to have captured all of the major meaningful groups of customer needs (segments). Moreover, by using sound sampling practices, the projected estimates of segment sizes, opportunities, and other firmographic and preference data will be sufficiently reliable to support strategic, marketing, and sales decisions and applications at relatively low risk.

The only real disadvantage of the Deep Approach is the level of effort and resource required to implement it. However, it is important to note that the Deep Approach has enough flavors that it is within the reach of most medium-to-large businesses. A more detailed description of the minimum level of effort required for the Deep Approach will give you a better understanding of the necessary resources.

Phase 1: Rigorous Qualitative Research

Broadly speaking, this phase of research has three objectives:

- definition of the relevant categories and subcategories of needs for your markets
- identification of the needs within each category and sub-category
- specification of the relevant firmographics

A word to the wise: This phase is the backbone of the segmentation. To get it right, your team must develop a highly disciplined and systematic mind-set that focuses not only on the forest but also on the trees. Remember, needs are not easily discovered. They do not always lurk near the surface. It takes a seasoned eye and tested interviewing techniques to uncover them. The lessons we have learned in conducting this first phase of segmentation research suggest some best practices that can help you master the process.

Best Practices for Conducting Qualitative Research

We recommend that qualitative research be conducted in an iterative fashion among a series of small but representative sets of current and potential customers. In contrast to the "big bang" technique, which relies on a single qualitative effort to identify a laundry list of needs, the iterative approach breaks down the exploratory research into two or more stages, each designed to test, validate, and refine knowledge acquired in the previous stage. The advantages of the iterative approach include a smaller, more discriminating set of needs; more precise, reliable definitions of market properties, such as decision-making structures, sizing units, and behavioral characteristics; and, finally, a sharper, more efficient, and focused questionnaire for use in the Phase 2 survey.

To operationalize the iterative approach, you begin by developing a representative list of current and potential customers. This list is then divided into several small but representative cross sections, one for use in each stage. In the first stage, your objective is to conduct a series of exploratory interviews with appropriate representatives of a hypothesized set of influence domains. Among other things, these interviews will produce a preliminary list of needs relative to each domain of influence. Building on the findings from the first-stage interviews, you then develop and administer a structured series of questions designed to test and validate the customer expressions of need in Stage 2. Complemented by an exploratory line of inquiry, structured questions will allow you to efficiently harvest the most important and potentially differentiating needs and behaviors. If, at the end of the second stage, uncertainties remain about needs, domains of influence, or other pertinent information, you may want to conduct an additional iteration of qualitative research to obtain closure.

Within these stages of Phase 1 there are a series of best practices we suggest that you follow. These include:

1. Develop a rigorous sample of organizations that best represents the relevant market.

Make sure you have adequate coverage of potential discriminators (e.g., industry, size, and product usage). Divide the proposed sample of organizations into replicates or cross sections — one for each stage.

2. Exercise care in preparing interviewing materials.

In addition to screening questionnaires for recruiting the appropriate respondents, you will need letters of introduction, topic guides, and, eventually, brief, structured questionnaires for testing and refining needs, as well as other important concepts.

3. Make sure you interview knowledgeable representatives for each of the domains of influence.

The framework provides you with a road map for identifying the types of people you will need to talk to within customer organizations. Plan on interviewing several individuals for each selected organization; as a general rule, start at the top of the target function group and use this first contact to identify the additional participants.

Although the interviews can be conducted by telephone, we get the best results in person. We find that face-to-face contact creates rapport and trust, which in turn produces more candid and less superficial responses. In addition, personal contact enables the interviewer to observe facial expressions, as well as body language, and to use these as cues for probes that we find often uncover important underlying needs and requirements.

Generally speaking, face-to-face interviews conducted at the customer site are most appropriate for senior-level executives and participants representing very large organizations. Site-based interviews are less threatening to participants. Familiarity with the turf and a feeling of control tend to facilitate open, in-depth communications. Moreover, concerns about the confidentiality of shared information are more readily reconciled when the participant can make eye-to-eye contact with the interviewer.

For some types of customers, focus groups are a cost-effective alternative to in-person on-site interviews. In our experience, focus groups produce effective results when participants are not concerned that a detailed discussion of needs will reveal strategically sensitive information. For the most part, midsize and small customers competing in markets with large numbers of competitors are good candidates for focus groups. In addition, functional buyers among even the largest firms tend to be candid and substantive when discussing needs in a group setting managed by a knowledgeable, experienced focus group moderator.

4. Use knowledgeable peer-level interviewers.

Among the most critical contributors to success in the qualitative phase is the selection of interviewers. We find that when the interviewers have been trained in exploratory interviewing techniques, exhibit comfortable familiarity with content, and are perceived as possessing acceptable peer-like status, interviews produce a deeper understanding of needs influencing behaviors. When these properties are not possessed by the interviewers, the results tend to be superficial and potentially misleading.

As an addendum to this point, we have found that client understanding of needs is enhanced when client team members participate directly in these interviews. However, if clients participate in the interviews, ethics require that the participants be informed prior to the interview. Such a revelation raises the issue of whether the results are biased. While every situation must be evaluated on its merits, our experience suggests that once the interview begins, participants tend to be honest and unbiased when describing needs.

5. Prepare a plan for analyzing the results.

When you develop the interviewing materials, create an initial analytic plan that maps questions to objectives. Review and refine the plan at the end of each stage.

At the conclusion of Phase 1, you should have filled in the framework for your markets. At minimum, you should have specified the categories and subcategories of need, defined the needs at each domain of influence, and identified relevant firmographics, including those you will use for sizing the segments.

Phase 2: Quantitative Research

Although you may want to add to this menu, the quantitative research has four primary objectives:

- segmenting the market
- determining the size of each segment
- evaluating opportunities by segment
- analyzing the segments

Since the data you gather in this phase will be used to support significant product development, as well as critical strategic and tactical marketing and sales decisions, it is crucial that you apply "best practices" when conducting the quantitative research.

Best Practices for Conducting Quantitative Research

Building on our experience, here are some suggested best practices that will help you get the most out of your research.

1. Create a plan for analyzing results in conjunction with questionnaire development.

An analytic plan should specify objectives and map specific questions to objectives. Once this mapping is in place, specific types of analyses should be identified and tied to questions and objectives. For example, if opportunity sizing is an objective, what questions will be asked to reliably size opportunities by segments, and what specific analytic techniques will be used to measure opportunities by segment.

One useful method for testing and validating the analytics prior to fielding the questionnaire is to create straw men. These straw men consist of hypothesized findings and segments. Once you have created these data, use them to demonstrate how the results will satisfy the objectives. A spin-off benefit of this exercise is the detection of gaps between objectives and data as well as areas of overkill.

2. Select an unbiased, comprehensive, and current list of businesses for sampling.

After eight years and hundreds of business market surveys, we have concluded that commercial lists such as those compiled by Dun & Bradstreet and Trinet, while not perfect, are the best available sources of business customer sample. If you want to include government and education markets in your segmentation, you will have to supplement these lists. In addition, some of our clients match their own customers against samples drawn from these lists to ensure that a cross section of their customers is represented in the sample.

3. Design and test the sizing plan before you draw samples.

The quick road to disaster is to wait until after you have collected data to figure out how you will project the results to your entire market. The best advice we can offer is to develop a weighting model as you design the sampling plan. Once you develop the plan, test it with some hypothetical numbers to make sure it works.

4. Make sure the sampling plan is flexible enough to account for diverse decision-making styles and robust enough to yield and inspire confidence in the statistics gathered.

One of the challenges faced by a survey design for the business market is the diversity of decision-making styles. For instance, there are decentralized and centralized forms of decision making. Within these two broad categories, there are numerous variations, often depending on the nature of the purchase. An effective method for covering diverse forms of decision making is to use the establishment or location, rather than the company or enterprise, as the primary sampling unit. This allows you to discover the right decision maker regardless of form and, at the same time, preserve the integrity of projectability.

To create sampling efficiencies and protect against overrepresentation of small customers and underrepresentation of larger customers, you will want to stratify your sample using a disproportionate design. Remember, more than 80 percent of all business establishments have fewer than 20 employees.

Our rule of thumb for sample size is that you will want a minimum of 70 completed interviews in each segment. Because the segments are not equally represented in the market, you will need to overcompensate on sample to pick up enough of the lower incidence segments to complete your analysis.

Depending on your markets and the level of statistical confidence you feel comfortable with, you will need to complete between 300 and 1500 interviews.

5. Test screening techniques to be certain you interview qualified respondents.

Since the framework is designed to capture the needs of multiple sources of influence on a purchase decision, you will need to establish a screening questionnaire to identify and qualify survey participants based on their ability to represent reliably the needs of one or more domains of influence. Our experience suggests that the telephone interview is the most efficient and effective vehicle for qualifying respondents. Also, we have found that the most appropriate entry point is the target functional unit, simply because individuals in those units are likely to be sympathetic and cooperative in helping you locate a reliable source to assess strategic and operations needs. In most cases, a single individual will be a reliable source for all categories of needs or will internally coordinate completion of the questionnaire by other knowledgeable sources.

6. The most effective and efficient data collection methods are telephone calls followed by mail or in-person interviewing.

Although the telephone is the most cost-effective and reliable method for screening, it is not a reliable method for data collection. Since you can expect 15 to 25 needs-related questions for each category, we have found that when the telephone is used to administer these questions, respondents become fatigued, and the reliability of the responses deteriorates. In our experience, the use of telephone screening to qualify and obtain cooperation, followed by a mail questionnaire, provides the best trade-off between cost and reliability. While in-person interviewing promises the optimal reliability, it can become very expensive to administer.

7. Strict quality controls are necessary during the data collection period.

Given the value of reliable data to strategic planning, product development, marketing, and sales planning, you cannot compromise reliability with lax quality controls on data collection. To ensure quality control, we recommend that you adopt the following techniques:

- rigorous pretesting of the screening questionnaires
- training of screening interviewers
- listen-in monitoring of the screening itself
- establishing sample control procedures
- monitoring the firmographic characteristics of returns for nonresponse bias
- conducting follow-up reminder calls if necessary to correct for observed nonresponse bias
- validating at least 10 percent of the responses to ensure a qualified respondent completed the interview

8. Equally strict quality controls are required during the data processing phase.

The reliability of the analyses can be adversely affected by dirty data; that is, respondent recording errors or erroneously entered data. To avoid these errors, all returned questionnaires should be thoroughly edited and key entries 100 percent verified.

9. Factor and cluster analyses are the preferred statistical procedures for segmenting customers.

You will have a choice among several statistical procedures for segmenting the market. Among these are correspondence analysis, principal-components analysis, and factor-cluster analysis. In our experience, correspondence analysis and principal-components analysis often lose a substantial amount of differentiation between segments — they oversimplify. Because we have found this additional differentiation to be valuable, we prefer the more rigorous factor-cluster method.

At the end of the analytic stage, you will have specified your segments, estimated the size and opportunity within and across segments, and defined the firmographic characteristics of the segments.

BUDGET APPROACHES

While the Deep Approach for creating the benchmark needs-based segmentation can be completed cost effectively, some businesses, particularly new, small, or financially constrained businesses, may not have the financial resources to fully implement the Deep Approach. Because most of these businesses can benefit by using the MBS framework, we feel compelled to provide some low-cost options for completing the benchmark segmentation effort.

The Do-It-Yourself Option

It is possible to accomplish the objectives of the Deep Approach by using internal resources to do most of the work in the qualitative and quantitative phases. External expertise can be limited to advice and training, questionnaire construction, sampling, telephone screening, data processing, and statistical analyses. Internal resources can be used to recruit and conduct in-depth qualitative interviews in Phase 1, interpret Phase 1 outcomes, and translate them into a design for the study — both questionnaire and sample designs — and to interpret, analyze, and draw conclusions from Phase 2 results.

Regardless of the mix of internal and external resources you use, we strongly recommend that you closely follow the best practice guidelines cited earlier. These guidelines are designed to help you produce results that are sufficiently reliable to support the use of the benchmark segmentation information for crucial strategic and tactical applications.

The Qualitative Phase-Only Option

If you select this approach, you will conduct only the Phase 1 qualitative research and use these directional data to make judgments about the presence, structure, and size of segment opportunities. If you are willing to accept the limitations cited earlier, there are several legitimate variations in the Phase 1 approach that can be used. For example, you can use focus groups rather than in-depth, in-person interviews and realize some reductions in the cost of Phase 1. Alternatively, you can use internal staff to conduct the in-depth, in-person interviews in Phase 1. If you choose the latter option, make sure these individuals are fully trained in objective needs-oriented interviewing techniques.

The primary advantage of using only qualitative research is that it provides a directional diagnostic about market needs and potential needs-based groupings of customers at a low cost. However, it is important to remember that if you do not conduct a survey using rigorous sampling and survey procedures, your needs diagnostics and assumptions about the presence, structure, and sizes of segments can be inaccurate if not totally misleading. Without the sound statistical basis for evaluating the degree of inaccuracy provided by quantitative research, your conclusions may only be tentative.

Nonetheless, if you follow the best practices for conducting qualitative research described earlier and recognize the limitations of the results, the qualitative research can be a valuable, low-cost method for creating the benchmark information that is necessary to support the strategic and tactical applications described in Chapters 5 and 6. Qualitative data may be very helpful in the hands of experts, managers, and decision makers as a component of their analyses in devising a market understanding — such an approach is illustrated in the Champion example of de Kluyver and Whitlark described in Chapter 2.

We do not recommend that you save money by skipping the qualitative phase and conducting only the quantitative survey. In our judgment, such a strategy produces data that have the appearance of statistical properties (e.g., statistical confidence intervals and projectability) but are misleading. Without input from a reasonably representative group of customers to guide development of the needs-based questions in the questionnaire, you face considerable risk of missing important and discriminating needs.

5

STRATEGIC APPLICATIONS

Whether you are large or small, sell computers or electricity, operate in domestic or global markets, building a business in the 1990s will be difficult. According to a survey we conducted for the *Wall Street Journal*, most CEOs expect their markets to become more competitive. But what appears to concern CEOs most is not the prospect of more competition, rather it is the form the competition is expected to take. The future they describe and the prescriptions for survival they offer send a profound message to those who will be responsible for strategy development in the 1990s.

THE VISION OF THE FUTURE MARKETPLACE

There is a virtual consensus among business leaders worldwide that national markets will become more crowded, as well-financed multinational corporations increase the pace of globalization in search of customers. Market crowding will be amplified by technology evolution.

Technology is expected to change more rapidly and to become more sophisticated, less expensive, and easier to duplicate. Under these conditions, the range of available product choices will become so extensive that no one supplier will be able to be all things to all buyers. Most leaders believe that a primal urge to physically differentiate products will force competitors into faster cycles of product-line extension and new product development. Growth in product-line extensions will radically expand the number of products in the competitive arena, while shorter product cycles will impose higher costs on producers. Following simple laws of economics, business leaders conclude that profit margins will decrease as excess supply forces prices down and shorter product life cycles push product costs up.

While the big guys are slugging it out in an increasingly smaller arena at lower profits, the availability of technology at lower costs will encourage small, agile companies to nibble markets by developing temporary niches. The entry of large numbers of smaller businesses into an already crowded market will produce unprecedented fragmentation — an environment in which the customer becomes king.

You do not have to search very hard to find evidence supporting this vision. Take a quick look at the computer markets in which IBM faces global competition from Hitachi and NEC while smaller competitors such as Amdahl and Compaq nibble at niches. Alternatively, there is the long-distance market in which AT&T, MCI, and US Sprint are expanding an increasingly price-sensitive struggle for customers beyond U.S. boundaries. Or in the cellular market, regional telephone companies such as Bell Atlantic, BellSouth, Pactel, and US West are attempting to establish market presence in Europe, Asia, and South America while simultaneously investing heavily in product extensions with data and fax features in an effort to differentiate themselves from smaller domestic providers.

THE PRESCRIPTION

For large and small companies alike, the 1990s will be unforgiving. Errors will be costly and potentially fatal in fast-moving markets. Unlike previous decades, few will succeed for long on genius, inspiration, or breakthrough technologies alone. According to business leaders such as Jack Welch of General Electric, George Fisher of Motorola, and Alain Gomez of Thomson S.A., winning on a sustained basis in the volatile 1990s will require the effective implementation of just-in-time product development and marketing strategies. To work, these strategies must deliver products and services customers want, when they want them, and in the diverse forms they want them.

But successful implementation in highly competitive, fragmented markets will present serious challenges. Obviously, the potential for mistakes will be increased by the push for a fast response in markets that are becoming more complex. Moreover, market risks will be compounded in the 1990s, as evolving competitive capabilities make the marketplace less forgiving.

So, how can you minimize the risks, get the right product mix to the right markets at the right time, and generate acceptable margins? According to Welch, Fisher, and Gomez, successful companies will achieve these objectives by establishing a disciplined process for accurately monitoring their customers' pulse, rapidly selecting markets of opportunity, and quickly responding to customer needs in these opportunity markets with a targeted mix of products that appears to be customized yet leverages core product components.

To operationalize this just-in-time prescription, you must adopt an integrated, stepwise strategic process that incorporates the following activities:

- timely, accurate monitoring of evolving customer needs
- identification of customer segments with similar needs
- sizing the opportunities these segments represent
- selecting target opportunity segments that are consistent with your capabilities and profit objectives
- developing and delivering products and services that effectively satisfy the needs of these target segments
- creating competitive positioning strategies around the needs these products and services were designed to address
- educating the field force
- executing related sales and service strategies

Because the needs-based MBS framework permits you to systematically identify patterns of customer needs, it is an effective platform for integrating these strategic activities. Beginning with the use of the framework as the cornerstone for monitoring and analyzing the structure of your markets over time, you can employ a step-by-step process for applying the MBS framework to build an integrated, disciplined strategy for getting it right in the 1990s. Exhibit 21 outlines these steps.

---

1. Conduct a Market-Structure Analysis

Building and refreshing a profile of your markets is the foundation on which winning strategies and tactics will be constructed in the 1990s. These market profiles provide the benchmark database that supports all subsequent analytics. As such, they must comprehensively and accurately answer the following questions:

- **Who Are Your Buyers?**
  This is a descriptive profile of the current and potential customer base, which includes your customers as

Exhibit 21
STEP-BY-STEP
STRATEGIC APPLICATIONS

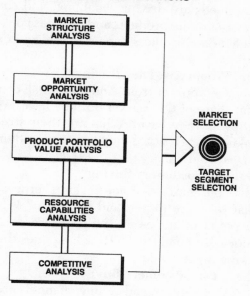

well as your competition's customers. These descriptions must capture relevant information such as industry type, number of locations, and number of employees.

- **What Are They Buying?**
This is a profile of relevant product and service inventories; that is, what *core* and *extended* products and services are currently used, how many, and from what suppliers? What *core* products and services as well as *extensions* are likely to be acquired in the near future, how many, and from what suppliers?

103

- **Why Do Customers Buy the Products and Services They Buy?**
  What needs are driving, enabling, and constraining purchases of the products and services you sell? What benefits do customers expect to realize as a result of purchase?
- **From Whom Are They Buying?**
  Who are your current and potential competitors? What share of the market do they have? What capabilities do they have? What are their strengths and weaknesses? How are they positioning themselves to their customers?
- **How Are Customers Buying?**
  What purchase decision-making processes exist? What roles are played and by whom? What are the sources of influence on the purchase decision? And under what conditions? How long does the decision-making process take?
- **Where Do Customers Buy?**
  What distribution and selling channels are used and preferred? Direct? Third parties or intermediaries?
- **When Do Customers Buy?**
  Under what conditions do customers make new buys or rebuys?

Why is a database profiling the structure of the market so critical to winning in the future? Simple. To win on a sustained basis in the highly fragmented, fast-moving markets of the future, you will have to quickly and correctly anticipate and respond to market changes. A comprehensive market-structure database that is routinely updated gives you an early warning system that can help you diagnose problems accurately, respond quickly to changes in customer needs and buying behaviors, and meet competitive challenges.

However, to capitalize on the advantages of a market-structure analysis, there are three rules of thumb you must follow.

- **First and foremost, the initial benchmark data collection activity must be comprehensive.**
  Virtually every business we know collects and maintains information on the structure of its markets. Unfortunately, these databases are almost always shallow and incomplete. The common practice is to profile markets using readily available descriptive information such as SIC and size. In some cases, product and service inventory data are maintained for customers. Similar data for competitors' customers are missing or incomplete. Few, if any, companies routinely and systematically monitor market needs. As a consequence, these databases cannot be used to swiftly and correctly detect changes in market needs and behaviors. And equally important, they are unable to support low-risk strategies and tactics that are responsive to these changes.

- **Second, the benchmark database must be routinely updated in time to support strategic planning and product development cycles.**
  If the primary motivation for conducting market-structure analysis is to detect and diagnose changes in market needs and behaviors, then it is critical that benchmark data be updated periodically. While the frequency of these updates will depend on the pace of change in your markets, nonetheless some form of progressive refreshment is essential. Equally important, data must be gathered and processed in time, so they can be used effectively by strategic planners and product developers.

- **Third, simple, unifying analytics are required to support strategic and tactical integration between product development, marketing, and sales.**
The major risk of investing in a comprehensive market-structure analysis is that you become paralyzed, not only by the sheer magnitude of the data, but also by different interpretations the data might foster. To avoid paralysis and force integration, you need a simple, unifying analytic framework that supports a quick, unambiguous diagnosis and response to changes in the market. By focusing on needs-based segments, the MBS framework allows you to reduce a complex database into a simple, unified structure for strategic and tactical integration of product development, marketing, and sales. Let us show you how.

BUILDING THE DATABASE

The most cost-effective method for constructing a database to support reliable yet comprehensive market-structure analyses is to use the benchmark needs-based segmentation survey as a starting point. By following the steps we described in Chapters 3 and 4, you can produce a reliable database that is representative of, and projectable to, the entire market. By including questions in the survey that capture data on the key market-structure elements we identified earlier in this chapter, the database can contain the information you need to support comprehensive market-structure analyses. Alternative and frequently more expensive methods, such as the merger of D&B business census data with customer billing, sales, or service records, fail to produce much of the information you need, not only about your own customers, but also about your competitors' customers and your potential markets.

Once the benchmark data are collected, you can segment your market using the MBS framework. The segmentation can divide your market into groups or segments of customers with similar needs related to business strategy, business operations, and the relevant target functions. Remember, each segment will have a portfolio of needs that differs from other segments.

After you have defined the segments, you will want to construct profiles of each segment by simply cross tabulating key market-structure data from the survey with the segments. Exhibit 22 illustrates in abbreviated form what these profiles might look like.

Each year after the benchmark survey, you will need to conduct a survey containing a subset of the questions used in the benchmark study. The purpose of this annual tracking survey is to refresh your database. It is our experience that segment sizes will change gradually over time; however, the structure of the segmentation will remain stable over a five- to ten-year period, unless there is a major change in the environment, such as a deep recession or a major technology shift. Nonetheless, the structure of the segmentation should be checked every three to five years.

Given the significant contribution the market-structure database can make to your annual strategic-planning efforts, it is imperative that you conduct these tracking surveys in advance of your planning cycle so that you have sufficient time to process and analyze the information.

How to Use Market-Structure Analysis

The market-structure analysis will become the key reference database for almost all subsequent strategic planning efforts. Virtually all your strategic decisions related to the

Exhibit 22
MARKET STRUCTURE PROFILE

MARKET STRUCTURE ELEMENTS	OVERALL MARKET	MBS SEGMENTS					
		1	2	3	4	5	6
WHO (TOTAL ENTERPRISES)							
• INDUSTRY TYPE (SIC)							
- MANUFACTURING	25%	30%	10%	5%	20%	15%	20%
- DISTRIBUTION	12%	10%	30%	10%	20%	5%	25%
- FINANCIAL	15%	5%	15%	35%	10%	20%	15%
- OTHER	48%	55%	45%	50%	50%	60%	35%
• AVERAGE SIZE (Expenditures in last FY for relevant equip.)	$2 billion	$200 MM	$300 MM	$500 MM	$100 MM	$800 MM	$100 MM
WHAT							
• PRODUCT PENETRATION (% of all eligible locations)							
- PBX	65%	40%	50%	75%	30%	80%	30%
- MULTIPLEXER	25%	15%	20%	25%	25%	45%	25%
- MODEMS	25%	45%	30%	20%	25%	15%	25%
• INSTALLED BASE (in # of units)							
- PBX	650,000	65,000	97,500	162,500	65,000	227,500	32,500
- MULTIPLEXER	350,000	35,000	52,500	87,500	35,000	122,500	17,500
- MODEM	250,000	87,500	62,500	12,500	37,500	25,000	37,500
WHY (NEEDS)							
• STRATEGIC							
- QUALITY	◐	●	○	○	●	○	●
- PRICE	◐	○	●	●	○	●	○
- INNOVATION	◑	●	○	●	○	○	○
• OPERATIONS							
- GROW SKILL BASE	◑	●	○	○	●	○	○
- INCREASE PRODUCTIVITY	◐	○	●	●	○	●	●
- IMPROVE PERFORMANCE	◐	●	○	●	●	●	●
• TELECOM MANAGEMENT							
- STANDARDIZE	◐	●	○	●	●	○	●
- CENTRALIZE	◕	●	○	●	●	●	○
- COST CONTROL	◐	●	●	○	○	○	●

108

Exhibit 22 (Cont.)

ILLUSTRATIVE

MARKET STRUCTURE ELEMENTS	TOTALS	MBS SEGMENTS					
		1	2	3	4	5	6
COMPETITIVE ANALYSIS							
• SHARE (PBX)							
- VENDOR A	42%	45%	30%	40%	35%	50%	20%
- VENDOR B	39%	25%	30%	50%	45%	35%	55%
- VENDOR C	19%	30%	40%	10%	20%	15%	25%
• PERCEIVED STRENGTHS (A)							
- PRICE	●	●	●	●	○	●	○
- SERVICE	◐	●	◐	◐	○	○	●
- QUALITY	◐	○	◐	○	◐	◐	●
• PERCEIVED WEAKNESSES (A)							
- PRICE	○	○	○	○	○	○	●
- SERVICE	◐	○	◐	◐	◐	◐	●
- QUALITY	●	●	◐	●	○	●	●
BUYING PROCESS (PBX)							
• KEY INFLUENCERS							
- SENIOR EXECS	◕	●	◐	◐	◐	○	●
- TELECOM MGT.	◕	◐	●	●	◐	●	○
• ROLES (Telecom Mgt.)							
- RECOMMEND	●	◐	●	●	●	●	●
- FINAL DECISION	◐	○	◐	◐	○	●	○
• PURCHASE CYCLE (Average)	6 mos.	5 mos.	7 mos.	4 mos.	8 mos.	3 mos.	5 mos.
CHANNEL PREFERENCE							
- DIRECT	◕	◐	●	●	○	●	○
- MAIL/TELEPHONE	◔	●	○	○	●	○	○
- INTERMEDIARY	●	●	◐	◐	●	○	●
PRODUCT PURCHASE PROPENSITY							
- CURRENT	◐	◐	◐	◐	○	○	○
- EXTENSIONS	◕	●	●	●	○	●	○
- NEW PRODUCT	●	●	●	●	●	●	○

● HIGH
◐ MEDIUM
○ LOW

market, including market selection, product development, and the definition of your product portfolio, as well as your competitive positioning, will be guided by your analysis of the segment profiles. These profiles will be used to estimate revenue and profitability potential by segment. Beyond the financials, you will want to assess your capabilities for serving each segment and to evaluate competitive strengths and weaknesses. These analyses will help you determine the markets where you should concentrate your product development, marketing, and sales planning activities. Importantly, these strategic target segments will serve as a simple, easy-to-understand platform for integrating product development, marketing, and sales. In the remaining sections, we describe how you can use the MBS framework and the market-structure database to assess and select markets, define new product opportunities, and design advantaged competitive positionings.

2. Analyze Market Opportunities

Should we enter the European market? Should we invest in the development of a new product line? Should we extend our current product line? Should we close out an existing product line? Should we exit a market?

At the heart of the answers to these questions is an assessment of the opportunities and risks associated with the alternatives. What is the revenue potential? How much will it cost us? What profit margins can we expect? Is the timing right? Do we have the technical and human resource capabilities to capitalize on the opportunity? What capabilities does the competition have? How will the competition respond? These are among the most critical issues business strategists must wrestle with while they attempt to evaluate opportunities and risks.

Given the stakes, we doubt that many businesses treat these issues lightly. Nevertheless, our findings suggest that the quality and rigor of their analysis is often flawed. In surveys we conducted in the mid-1970s and early 1980s among executives representing some of the leading companies in the United States, we discovered a rather consistent pattern in rates of failure among new product offerings. Approximately two out of three new product offerings did not realize projected revenues and profits, and as a consequence, they were withdrawn from the market. The most commonly cited reason for the failures was the lack of adequate research to evaluate the acceptability of the products to the market. Even if we assume some improvement in new product success rates as a function of learning, failure rates of between 30 to 50 percent in the volatile 1990s will prove disastrous.

More important, if new product failure rates approach 50 percent, it is likely that market selection and product-line extension failure rates will also be above acceptable levels. We think a more systematic analysis of the opportunities using the needs-based market structure data can help you reduce the risks of failed market selection and product offerings.

Evaluating Opportunities Using the MBS Framework

The prudent method for developing a market strategy that minimizes the risk of failure and maximizes your ability to capitalize on opportunities involves a disciplined and systematic assessment of the current and future revenues, costs, and net profitability for each segment by current product, planned product extensions, and potential new product offerings. Such an assessment can be used to guide overall market selection and target market decisions for current products, planned product-line extensions, as well as potential new product offerings.

To complete these analyses you must gather the following types of information in the benchmark needs-based segmentation survey:

- the number of currently installed units by product category and vendor
- estimates of the number of units that will be acquired, replaced, or abandoned over the next two years by product and vendor
- the probability of purchasing product-line extensions you are considering, including the number of units to be acquired and the preferred vendor (participants are asked to respond to brief concept statements)
- the probability of acquiring new products being considered for development, including the likely number of units and the preferred vendor (although brief concept statements can be used, more sophisticated and elaborate techniques for measuring acquisition likelihood — such as conjoint or trade-off analysis — are preferred, because the data are more useful in guiding product development)

These benchmark data must be updated annually using the tracking survey described later in this chapter.

You will need to supplement the benchmark and tracking data with estimates of the average dollar value of each unit to calculate expected revenues. You can obtain these data by using internal resources to estimate an average cost per installed unit, or you can ask each survey participant to estimate the cost of installed products, as well as anticipated annual expenditures. One advantage of using both techniques is that you can verify your internal estimates of revenues with survey participant estimates and vice versa.

In addition, you will need to estimate the amortized cost of product development, marketing, and sales for each product and vendor by segment. Although this is a challenging task, it is essential to the calculation of profitability. Even a rough guess is better than no information on the differential cost of providing products to each segment. In our experience, segments will vary on the cost to serve. Typically, this variance is due to differences across segments in selling cycles, product customization, service requirements, and geographic dispersion.

With these data in hand, you will be ready to evaluate opportunities and risks within each segment with the goal of gaining an overall assessment by market. An example reveals the strategic value of systematic opportunity analysis using the MBS framework.

AN OPPORTUNITY ANALYSIS SAMPLE

Let us assume for a moment that you are a manufacturer of PBXs and you have conducted a benchmark needs-based segmentation in the United States. Since you are currently considering several extensions to your PBX product line, you included in the benchmark survey brief concept statements describing the new features, as well as several prices for the feature extensions to test price sensitivity.

In addition, you are thinking about a new PBX product for PC-based local-area networks. To determine if there is a sufficient market to warrant introduction of this product and obtain information on how best to design, package, and price it, you included a conjoint sort task in the survey. (See Exhibit 30 in Chapter 6 for an outline of the process of conjoint analysis.) This sort task asks participants to evaluate alternative configurations of the product offering, including price and vendor. Based on the results of the sort task, you will know the relative contribution of each feature to a preference for the product. These data can be used to model the demand, revenue, and shares for alternative product packages in different competitive situations.

In preparation for strategic planning and product development activities, your first step is to construct a market-structure profile similar to Exhibit 22. Among the information elements in the market-structure analysis is a profile of the number of current PBX units and expenditures by vendor for the market as a whole, as well as for each segment. And, because you asked about future purchases, you have estimates of the number of add-on, replacement, and new purchases by vendor and segment over the next two years. Exhibit 23 profiles the current and near-future PBX revenues by vendor and segment for the U.S. market. Before you continue your analysis, you will verify the survey estimates against your sales data. If a discrepancy exists, you will recalibrate your overall share of total units and revenues and then proportionately adjust competitor units and revenues.

At this point in the analysis, the revenue data indicate that the preponderance of your current revenues comes from Segments 3 and 5. Your primary competitor gets most of its revenues from the same segments. Obviously, one or both of you is not doing an effective job of differentiation in the PBX marketplace. Even more important to your opportunity analysis is the alarming evidence that in the next two years almost all segments expect to purchase significantly fewer units than in the past, particularly Segments 3 and 5. Even though your primary competitor will experience a decline in revenues, the decline is not

Exhibit 23
OPPORTUNITY ANALYSES
(BASE CASE: ESTIMATED REVENUES)

MBS SEGMENTS

CATEGORIES	TOTAL REVS (Millions)	OVERALL VENDOR SHARE (Millions/%) A	B	C	1 SEGMENT SHARE	1 VENDOR SHARE A	B	C	2 SEGMENT SHARE	2 VENDOR SHARE A	B	C	3 SEGMENT SHARE	3 VENDOR SHARE A	B	C	4 SEGMENT SHARE	4 VENDOR SHARE A	B	C	5 SEGMENT SHARE	5 VENDOR SHARE A	B	C	6 SEGMENT SHARE	6 VENDOR SHARE A	B	C
EXISTING PRODUCT LINE (PBX)	$1,300																											
CURRENT DOLLARS		$546	$507	$247	$130	$58	$33	$39	$195	$59	$58	$78	$325	$130	$163	$33	$65	$23	$29	$13	$520	$260	$182	$78	$65	$13	$36	$16
%		42%	39%	19%	10%	45%	25%	30%	15%	30%	30%	40%	25%	40%	50%	10%	5%	35%	45%	20%	40%	50%	35%	15%	5%	20%	55%	25%
FUTURE (ADDS REPLACEMENTS, NEW BUYS IN NEXT TWO YEARS)	$750																											
DOLLARS		$260	$343	$147	$113	$45	$45	$23	$188	$75	$66	$47	$225	$68	$124	$33	$75	$23	$37	$15	$75	$34	$30	$11	$75	$15	$41	$19
%		35%	46%	19%	15%	40%	40%	20%	25%	40%	35%	25%	30%	30%	55%	15%	10%	30%	50%	20%	10%	45%	40%	15%	10%	20%	55%	25%

(A) YOUR SHARE

(O) IMPORTANT DIFFERENCES

115

Exhibit 24
OPPORTUNITY ANALYSES
(BASE CASE ESTIMATED PROFIT MARGINS)

CATEGORIES	TOTAL PROFIT (Millions)	OVERALL VENDOR PROFIT MARGINS			MBS SEGMENTS 1 SEGMENT MARGINS	1 VENDOR MARGINS			2 SEGMENT MARGINS	2 VENDOR MARGINS			3 SEGMENT MARGINS	3 VENDOR MARGINS			4 SEGMENT MARGINS	4 VENDOR MARGINS			5 SEGMENT MARGINS	5 VENDOR MARGINS			6 SEGMENT MARGINS	6 VENDOR MARGINS		
		A	B	C		A	B	C		A	B	C		A	B	C		A	B	C		A	B	C		A	B	C
EXISTING PRODUCT LINE (PBX)																												
CURRENT DOLLARS	$156	$76	$60	$20	$11	$6	$2	$3	$26.6	$13	$5.8	$7.8	$42	$11	$29	$2	$5.5	$2	$3	$.5	$66	$42	$18	$5	$4.9	$2	$2.2	$.7
%	12%	14%	12%	8%	8%	10%	6%	9%	14%	22%	10%	10%	13%	8%	18%	7%	8%	9%	10%	5%	13%	16%	10%	8%	7%	15%	6%	4%
FUTURE (ADDS, REPLACEMENTS, NEW BUYS IN NEXT TWO YEARS)																												
DOLLARS	$105	$42	$41	$22	$15	$8	$4	$3	$30	$19	$3	$8	$32	$6	$22	$4	$8	$2	$4	$2	$12	$5	$5	$2	$8	$2	$3	$35
%	14%	16%	12%	15%	14%	18%	9%	13%	16%	25%	9%	17%	14%	9%	8%	12%	11%	9%	11%	13%	16%	15%	17%	18%	13%	13%	7%	16%

Ⓐ YOUR SHARE

◯ IMPORTANT DIFFERENCES

116

likely to be as steep as yours. Clearly, a red flag is posted. Why will overall sales drop? Why will your sales slip faster than your competition's? What remedial action should you take? Moreover, that competitor will become the new share leader if you do nothing.

Before you leap to any strategic decisions about the market, it is critical to assess the costs associated with serving each market segment. Perhaps some segments are inherently unprofitable to serve and should therefore be left to the competitors. Because you included a sample of your own customers in the benchmark survey, you are now able to assign a cost for selling to and servicing customers in each segment. Overhead costs, such as product development and marketing, can also be allocated on a per-customer basis. Using the revenue and cost data, you can roughly estimate the relative profitability for each segment. Applying simple extrapolation, you can extend these estimates for each segment over the next two years. We should note that a more refined profitability analysis, which includes such values as volumes, competitive intensity, and pricing, would enhance your assessment of profitability.

Exhibit 24 shows estimated current and short-term future profit margins for each segment. Notice that Segments 2 and 5 are currently the most profitable segments. Even more important, over the next two years, Segment 2 will become your most profitable segment.

Given the prospect of significant declines in revenue and market share, you should complete a similar analysis for the proposed product-line extensions and new product offerings prior to a final market-selection decision. As Exhibit 25 illustrates, when the product-line extensions are added to the opportunity equation, the configuration of attractive target segments changes. If you offer the extensions in conjunction with your current product, you increase the number of opportunity segments from three to four. Moreover, the added revenue potential associated with product-line extensions indicates that you should begin developmental work on the product-line extensions. It is important to note that data on the relative attractiveness of these product-line extension opportunities are critical to your near-term survival. A close examination of the needs expressed by the segments will provide insight into long-range product development opportunities. An effective targeted response to these underlying market drivers is more fundamental to your

Exhibit 25
OPPORTUNITY ANALYSES
(EXTENSIONS TO EXISTING PRODUCTS)

CATEGORIES	TOTALS (Millions)	MBS SEGMENTS					
		①	②	③	4	⑤	6
PROJECTED REVENUES/PROFITS FOR EXISTING PRODUCT LINE							
REVENUES ($)	$260	$45	$75	$68	$23	$34	$15
PROFITS ($)	$42	$9	$19	$6	$2	$5	$2
EXTENSIONS TO EXISTING PRODUCT LINES							
REVENUES ($)	$385	$65	$85	$82	$42	$77	$34
PROFITS ($)	$36	$5	$10	$7	$4	$7	$2
TOTALS							
REVENUES ($)	$645	$110	$160	$150	$65	$111	$49
PROFITS ($)	$78	$14	$29	$13	$6	$12	$4

⚫ OPPORTUNITY SEGMENTS

Exhibit 26
OPPORTUNITY ANALYSES
- NEW PRODUCT IMPACT -

CATEGORIES	TOTALS (millions)	MBS SEGMENTS					
		①	②	③	④	⑤	6
PROJECTED REVENUES/PROFITS FOR EXISTING PRODUCT LINE							
REVENUES ($)	$184	$35	$60	$52	$12	$17	$8
PROFITS ($)	$34	$7	$17	$5	$1	$3	$1
PROJECTED REVENUES FOR EXTENSIONS TO EXISTING PRODUCT*							
REVENUES ($)	$261	$50	$70	$71	$21	$34	$15
PROFITS ($)	$24	$4	$8	$6	$2	$3	$1
PROJECTED REVENUES/PROFITS FOR NEW PRODUCTS**							
- BASIC PCLAN PBX							
REVENUES ($)	$180	$10	$45	$10	$60	$15	$40
PROFITS ($)	$22	$2	$4	$2	$8	$2	$4
- PRIMARY PCLAN PBX							
REVENUES ($)	$210	$85	$30	$20	$35	$30	$10
PROFITS ($)	$25	$10	$4	$2	$5	$3	$1
- ENHANCED PCLAN PBX							
REVENUES ($)	$250	$30	$20	$75	$15	$100	$10
PROFITS ($)	$19	$2	$2	$6	$1	$7	$1
TOTALS							
REVENUES ($)	$1,085	$210	$225	$228	$143	$196	$83
PROFITS ($)	$124	$25	$35	$21	$17	$18	$8

* YOUR PROJECTED REVENUES AND PROFITS
** ASSUMES NO COMPARABLE COMPETITIVE PRODUCT AVAILABLE

long-term success than a response to near-term product extension opportunities.

In any case, the results of a new product analysis suggest that you would have been premature in making market-selection decisions based on the opportunity analyses for your current products and the extensions alone.

As Exhibit 26 illustrates, the conjoint analysis and subsequent choice modeling reveal that the introduction of a new product, the PC LAN PBX with three extensions, the Basic, Primary, and Enhanced versions, will affect your existing product revenues negatively, but will expand your total market opportunities considerably. When you examine revenues and profits across your existing product line, extensions, and the proposed products, five segments emerge as potential targets: 2, 1, 3, 5, and 4.

Supplementing the financial-opportunity analysis with the needs data for each candidate target segment and the remaining data from the market-structure analysis gives you a rudimentary assessment of the opportunities and risks in the market. Continued monitoring of market needs and requirements and competitive moves will enable you to refine this assessment over time. Armed with these analyses, you can begin to develop optimal, low-risk strategies for product development, marketing, and sales. Remember these analyses are not a panacea. The critical cornerstones of success are rooted in execution. For instance, meeting development schedules, implementing effective field-sales-targeting activities, and creating differentiating marketing messages are essential ingredients of effective execution.

3. Complete Product Portfolio Value Analyses

Before you make final decisions about market selection, you should complete a product portfolio value analysis. Product portfolio value analysis (PPVA) tells you the mix of current and short-term future product offerings that could provide maximum revenues, profitability, and competitive advantage within and across segments.

The strategic benefits of product mix selection based on PPVA are substantial. In the first place, PPVA should serve as a major input to market selection. By netting the revenue, profitability, and competitive advantages for each of your current products by segment and then summarizing across segments, you can assess your overall opportunities and risks for the market as a whole. Second, because PPVA indicates which mix of products is most attractive, profitable, and competitively advantaged in each segment, you can use it to guide product marketing strategies within and across segments. Third, PPVA can be used in conjunction with the expressed needs of the segments and conjoint analysis to identify and estimate the value of gaps in your current product portfolio.

Also, PPVA can be used to produce more efficient and effective prospecting and selling. For example, knowledge about needs and the mix of products preferred by customers in each segment can be used by sales to improve cross-selling opportunities and target the content of prospecting and sales calls. In addition, management can help a product portfolio strategy become a reality by using the PPVA as a guide for establishing quotas and incentives for cross selling.

Conducting a PPVA

From an analytic prospective, PPVA is simply an extension of the opportunity analyses supplemented by a realistic assessment of your resource capabilities and competitive advantages. The primary data you need to complete the baseline PPVA come from the opportunity information described in the section above. Annual updates to the baseline PPVA can be completed using the opportunity data from needs-based tracking surveys. Moreover, if you conduct individual product-based research (such as conjoint studies or product concept testing) between the benchmark and annual tracking surveys, you can update your portfolio strategy by including questions designed to measure cannibalization.

To show you how a PPVA works, we will take you through the analysis by continuing with the example of the telecommunications equipment supplier we used earlier:

Step 1: Calculate Current Portfolio Revenue and Profitability

Using data from the benchmark needs-based segmentation survey, revenue and margin of profitability potential can be calculated for each product by each segment. In addition, a similar analysis should be completed for competitive products assuming appropriate levels of profitability.

Step 2: Compute Expected Portfolio Revenues and Profits

Again, using data from the benchmark needs-based segmentation survey, calculate expected revenues and profitability for each product in each segment for your products and your competitors'.* Now, compare these data with current estimates to calibrate growth for your products as competing products by segment.

Step 3: Evaluate the Impact of Potential New Product Introductions on Existing Portfolio Revenues and Profitability

Once you have evaluated the value of your existing portfolio, you will want to assess the impact of new product offerings and product-line extensions on the value of your portfolio by segment and across the segments. Since you were considering developing a PBX LAN at the time of the benchmark needs-based seg-

---

* The benchmark survey should obtain data on expected purchases in the near future for relevant products.

mentation survey, you should include a conjoint exercise in the survey. In addition to likelihood of purchase, you asked survey participants to tell you how they would alter planned purchases if the new product was available. When you combine the conjoint data with the data on altered purchases, you are able to estimate the enhanced value the new product will add to your portfolio. Exhibit 26 illustrates this process.

Step 4: Assess Capabilities and Allocate Resources
In our experience, few companies systematically evaluate their capabilities on a routine basis, particularly in relation to strategic segmentation and product portfolios. Yet the success of a strategy depends in large part on your ability to implement it. If you do not take time to accurately assess the nature and availability of the skill base necessary to develop and launch a new product in a timely manner, it is possible you will fail to get the right product to the market before the competition. At the same time, if you fail to accurately evaluate the resources needed to counteract expected declines in revenues from your existing portfolio in traditionally strong segments, you face the prospect of declining cash flows at a time when you need cash to support product development. For many, these problems are a constant reality.

Those who do attempt to systematically evaluate capabilities and allocate resources against strategic plans often have little concrete, objective data to support the investment trade-off decisions they must make. By conducting a PPVA in the context of the needs-based framework, you will get the objective data you need to assess the trade-offs associated with resource investments. For instance, in our example, you have concrete data on the compounded revenue and profitability potential of the new product introduction for the market as a whole, as well as for each segment. You have similar data for your current product portfolio without the new product. Together, these data can be used to guide decisions about short- and long-range product development, target marketing, sales, promotion, distribution channel resource capabilities, and investments.

Step 5: Evaluate Your Competitive Advantages

Finally, before making final commitments to strategic product, market, sales, and distribution channel plans, it is essential to review the financial data in the context of resources, the needs of potential target markets, and competitive strengths and weaknesses across product portfolios. At a minimum, the PPVA and the needs-based MBS framework can be used to identify the segments in which competition is growing or losing share, revenues, and profitability. In addition, you can compare the needs of segments with competitor portfolios to identify needs the competition is likely to be satisfying as well as needs they are not meeting. Obviously, you will want to conduct a similar analysis of your own strengths and weaknesses. Ultimately, these analyses will help you develop competitive positioning strategies and tactics.

Beyond these analyses, you will want to conduct an independent assessment of your competitors' product development activities and resource capabilities. Once you have gathered this competitive intelligence, you will want to assess the information in the context of the needs-based segments and your PPVA. The results of these analyses will be used to finalize target segment selection and subsequent resource commitments.

In summary, a PPVA completed in the context of the needs-based segmentation framework can be used to guide product development strategies, investment trade-off decisions, market entry and exit decisions, and target-segment selection decisions. Even more important, a PPVA identifies the right mix of products for the right markets at the right time within acceptable margins. To capitalize on this valuable information, you will need efficient, effective product development and introduction processes and procedures.

4. Select Markets and Target Segments

Once you have completed the market structure, opportunity, and PPVA for each of your potential markets, you are ready to make final market and target-segment selections.

MARKET SELECTION

The word *market* means many things to many people. To avoid confusion here, we define market as a group of customers who buy related products and services. These customers can be distributed across geographies, represent various sizes and industries, and possess different needs and requirements.

Since few, if any, businesses have the resources to pursue and be successful in all possible markets simultaneously, most businesses need to be selective about the markets in which to compete or from which to exit. In the highly competitive 1990s, the choice of alternative markets will expand to global dimensions, and adroit market selection will be critical to success, if not survival.

To effectively select markets, you need to answer five basic questions:

- Do we have products and services that meet the needs of the market?
- Does the market offer sufficient revenue potential?
- Does the market offer sufficient profit potential?
- Do we have the resources and capabilities to compete successfully within acceptable profit margins?
- When should we enter or exit the market?

The needs-based MBS framework supplemented by market-structure, opportunity, and portfolio analyses can help you answer these questions.

MATCHING PRODUCTS WITH MARKET NEEDS

Regardless of whether you are currently in a market or considering market entry, it is a good idea to compare the needs across all domains and segments of the MBS framework with the needs your product lines satisfy. The most effective method for doing this comparison is to consider your products or proposed products one at a time — independent of the segmentation results — and determine the needs within each domain of influence for each segment that your products satisfy. Such a product by segment assessment will enable a specific analysis of differentiating product-to-needs maps and facilitate identification of target segments by product. While we do not have a magic formula to evaluate compatibility, common sense would suggest that the stronger the match on the needs the market feels most strongly about, the stronger the support for market entry.

A more objective way to accomplish this task is to recruit focus groups representing each segment and have participants identify the needs they think the products satisfy. This matching exercise will help you verify the compatibility of your products with market needs and identify unmet needs that could signal gaps in your product line or new product opportunities. A similar process should be used to evaluate competitive products and services since success in the market is likely to be a function of relative, rather than absolute, satisfaction of needs.

ESTIMATING REVENUE OPPORTUNITIES AND PROFITABILITY POTENTIAL

"Orders of magnitude" is the most common method for estimating the revenue and profitability potential of a new market. This technique starts with an estimate of the number of potential customers from Dun & Bradstreet or government statistics (e.g., the total number of businesses with fewer than 50 employees) and then continues with numerous subjective assumptions about potential purchases by segment or industry, including growth rates, sales penetration, and competitive shares. The product of these assumptions is an "order of magnitude" estimate of potential revenue and profitability. The estimate is typically arrived at by triangulation or negotiated compromise based on the reasonableness of various assumptions. Nonetheless, the rates of new product failure suggest that the assumptions underlying such estimates are wrong more often than right. Obviously, a more reliable method is necessary.

While no method will be 100 percent accurate, we think the MBS approach will produce substantially more accurate estimates of potential revenue and profitability than the ballpark approach, because it can replace assumptions about likely purchase behaviors with estimates provided directly by the customer in the benchmark survey. Here is how the MBS approach works.

Step 1: Use the MBS Benchmark Survey Data to Calculate the Available Market

If you are considering entry into new markets with a product category that already exists, we would recommend that you add a series of questions related to purchase intent over the next two years. Customers who currently use the product category and intend to replace or purchase add-ons in the next two years should be asked the likelihood of their switching vendors, the number of units they would replace or acquire, and their preference for alternative suppliers. Of course, you should be one of the alternative suppliers included in the options. Customers who do not currently use the product category but intend to acquire the product in the next two years should be asked how many units they intend to acquire, their likelihood of acquiring these units, and their preference for alternative suppliers, including your brand.

As a general rule of thumb, we have found that customers tend to overestimate the number of units they will purchase. You can compensate for overestimation by using a conservative likelihood of purchase threshold.

If you are introducing a totally new product category into the market, you are advised to use a conjoint sort task that solicits preferences and purchase likelihoods for different product packages offered at various prices by different vendors. As we noted earlier, this technique will allow you to estimate revenue potential and shares for a core product as well as alternative scenarios for product-line extension.

Step 2: Estimate Revenue and Profit Potential

Once you have calculated the available market, you

compute revenues and profitability using the same techniques described in the opportunity section.

EVALUATING RESOURCE CAPABILITIES AND TIMING

Although it is tempting to make market-selection decisions based on revenue and profitability potential alone, we recommend that capabilities be evaluated first to determine whether you have the appropriate resources to apply in the necessary time frame to capture the available market. As we indicated earlier, the needs-based MBS framework can help more accurately gauge the resources required by forcing an evaluation of the product requirements, as well as the marketing, sales, and distribution channel needs of each segment. Unfortunately, there is no easy, objective formula for calibrating these resources. Instead, the data will have to be reviewed by segment to judiciously estimate the labor and capital required. Exhibit 27 illustrates a broad set of steps for evaluating capabilities.

The needs-based benchmark database can give you some direct guidance on the timing for market entry. Simply include a time frame as a context for purchase intentions in the benchmark survey, and you will have a directional measure indicating how many units are likely to be purchased within a designated time frame.

5. Target Segment Selection

Because the MBS approach to market selection requires a projection of overall market revenue, profitability, capability, and timing estimates on the basis of expected performance in each segment, a natural by-product of market-selection analyses is the identification of target segments. Once identified, actual selection of target segments must be conditioned on, among other things, strategic, risk, and availability considerations.

Once you have selected the market and the target segments, you can complete your strategic analyses by using the needs-based MBS benchmark data to develop competitive positionings for each product. Issues concerning positioning (generally tactical in nature) are addressed in Chapter 6.

Exhibit 27
CAPABILITIES EVALUATION WORKSTEPS

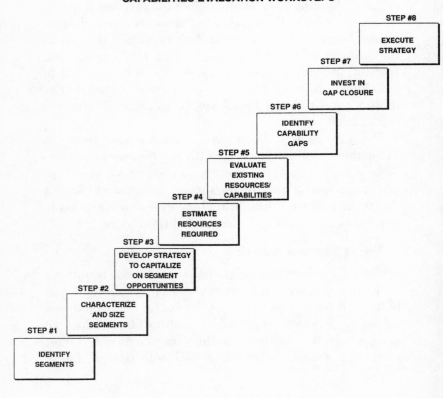

6. Integrate Needs-based Segmentation within Your Business Planning Process

While the MBS approach produces extremely powerful strategic analyses, these analyses can become a sterile exercise if they are not integrated into the business planning process. Integration offers important benefits. First, it forces you to think through the operational activities that are essential to successful implementation. Second, it helps you identify the areas where interaction and coordination among functional areas are essential. Third, it enables you to define, rectify, or reconcile organizational barriers to effective implementation. Finally, integration of the MBS framework within the business planning process encourages internal ownership, which is an essential ingredient to successful, coordinated pursuit of overall business objectives.

To help understand the importance of integration and provide some guidance on where and how to integrate the MBS approach into your business planning process, this chapter closes with a brief outline of a prototypical business planning process integrating the needs-based segmentation approach.

Clearly, no prototype can capture the complexity or variability that exists in organizational planning processes. However, we hope to identify primary activities and interactions in such a way that executives in large and small organizations alike can understand where and how the MBS approach can fit into their strategic planning.

THE STRUCTURE OF THE BUSINESS PLANNING PROCESS

As Exhibit 28 indicates, our business planning prototype has three major structures.

Exhibit 28
BUSINESS PLANNING PROCESS

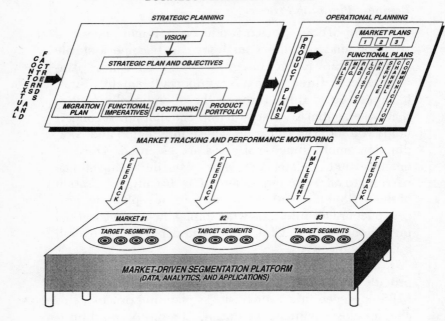

1. The Needs-based MBS Platform

This platform consists of an updated market-structure analysis complemented by analytics describing opportunities, product-portfolio values for selected markets, and needs-based segments within selected markets.

2. The Strategic Planning Process

The strategic planning process begins with a vision of the future position of the company, for example, "We will obtain share leadership by providing a mix of products and services that satisfy customer needs." This vision is guided by the needs-based market-selection and target-segment analytics, as well as contextual factors and trends — economic, political, regulatory, and technology barriers and conditions, for example. The vision is supported by a set of objectives related to how the organization will achieve its vision, what resources and capabilities will be required to achieve the vision, what competitive positioning is necessary, and what portfolio of products must be offered to the market.

3. The Operational Planning Process

Shaped by the strategic planning objectives, the operational plan is a specific, multiyear map that includes specific product, market, and functional action plans. These action plans are governed by detailed revenue-and-profit forecasts, schedules, budgets, technology, and logistics objectives and requirements for each segment within selected markets.

MONITORING SALES PERFORMANCE

Needs-based analytics are used to generate specific objectives for revenue, profitability, and cost by product for each segment within selected markets. To determine how well you are doing relative to plan objectives, it is essential that you establish mechanisms for monitoring performance on a monthly basis. Since the plan objectives are related to needs-based segments within selected markets, you will need to track sales, revenues, and costs by product within the needs-based segments.

To effectively track these values, your customers must be assigned to segments. There are two ways to do this: (1) develop a statistical equation that uses readily accessible firmographic information, that is, SIC, revenues, number of employees to estimate probabilities of customer membership in needs-based segments, or (2) administer a short set of needs-based segmentation questions in conjunction with prospecting or sales calls. Responses to the questions can be used to characterize the needs of specific customers "on the fly," permitting salespersons to customize a selling message according to each customer's needs. This second technique will be referred to as CLASSIFY™.

These monthly performance data can also be used to assess the effectiveness of various tactical activities such as sales, promotions, advertising, and distribution channels. Procedures for evaluating tactical performance will be discussed further in later chapters. In addition, the information systems required to track and monitor performance are described in Chapter 7.

To keep plans realistic and on track, it is essential that performance data be fed back into the operational plans in a timely manner so that plans and activities can be adjusted.

TRACKING NEEDS CHANGES

One of the critical success factors in the future will be the ability to respond quickly to market needs. The needs-based MBS approach provides you with the tools to track changes in needs on a routine basis.

As we have noted earlier, one of the products of the benchmark MBS survey can be a short-form CLASSIFY™ questionnaire. To keep tabs on evolving customer needs, you will need to periodically survey a representative sample of customers within your selected markets using the CLASSIFY™ questionnaire. To identify changing needs, you will want to supplement the existing CLASSIFY™ questions with open-ended questions designed to capture new, emerging needs. In addition, you may want to include questions about current product inventories or near-term purchase intentions to assess competitive penetration. Finally, these tracking surveys can be used as a vehicle to test interest in new product concepts or evaluate potential product-line extensions, pricing, or packaging ideas.

To ensure that your tracking surveys produce reliable results, we recommend the following guidelines:

- Regardless of whether you decide to track only your target segments or the entire market, you must be certain that the sample you survey is representative.
- Although the number of completed interviews will depend on the number of segments in your market, you should complete a minimum of 70 interviews per segment; 100 interviews per segment will yield greater statistical reliability.
- The frequency of tracking will depend on your financial resources and the instability of your markets. At a minimum, you should be tracking markets at least once a year; ideally, once a quarter.
- Data from tracking surveys can be folded into the benchmark data over time to create tighter statistical relationships (e.g., the relationship between firmographic characteristics and segment membership).

As is the case with sales performance monitoring, the results of the needs-tracking surveys should provide a timely, accurate snapshot of the market framed in a simple, easy-to-digest format. Armed with this snapshot, you will be prepared to act quickly to changes in the market.

FROM STRATEGY TO TACTICS

At this point, we have described how the MBS framework can be used as the cornerstone for the formulation of responsive business, marketing, and product strategies and plans. Nonetheless, the ultimate success of your business will depend on how well you execute in the trenches on a day-to-day basis. The next chapter describes how to use the needs-based approach on a tactical level to more effectively package and price products and services, design and execute promotions and advertising, and select and support sales and distribution channels. However, as preface to this discussion of tactical applications, it is important to realize that the ability to compete effectively is due in large part to effective translation of strategic plans to action in the field. To help you think through the process of translating strategy to tactics, we offer the following guidelines:

- **Everyone from the CEO to the sales and service staff in the field must sing from the same market-driven hymnal.**

To accomplish this feat, you must train, train, and train everyone in your organization to think and speak in terms of segments and needs. In time, this training will produce a market-driven culture, a uniform focus, and a more reliable translation of strategy to action.

- **Simplicity is a virtue.**

To reflect accurately the dynamics of the business market, it is necessary to use a complex framework; however, if the complexity cannot be captured in a simple, easy-to-understand map, it will not work. The simplifying feature of the needs-based approach is the segment structure. The labels you assign to these segments will take on a life of their own. Promote them. Organize and create incentives around them. But do not neglect the complex needs these labels represent. Of equal importance, do not forget the planning, monitoring, and tracking processes that are essential to keeping in sync with the market.

- **Create ownership.**

Since no one can be everywhere and do everything, plan execution will have to rely on the synchronized efforts of many

136

people. Effective delegation of the needs-based approach down the line requires the creation of ownership. Ownership requires confidence, trust, and a feeling of satisfaction. To foster these qualities, training and incentive programs need to be put into place from the highest to the lowest level in your organization.

- **Remain agile.**

Since success depends on quick response, do not create an overly layered decision-making structure around the needs-based approach. Use the information the approach generates. Set up quick-response communications channels with clear, direct feedback loops. Once training is complete, encourage individuals to act independently and creatively within broad guidelines. Periodic performance monitoring will ensure individual actions are compatible with strategic plans.

Overall, success in the marketplace requires sustained, proactive managerial leadership committed to the vision of an organization working as an integrated unit within the foundation of the needs-based MBS framework.

6

TACTICAL
APPLICATIONS OF MBS

If it was ever true that building a better mousetrap was sufficient to generate customer demand, those days are long past.
The difficulties of getting your message heard while producing
an attractive mousetrap at a competitive price are too formida-
ble to permit purely reactive marketing tactics.

In your initial strategic planning, you have used MBS to
analyze the market's structure and opportunities for your firm,
and to select the appropriate markets and target segments for
your products and services. In addition, you have considered
how your products and services can match market needs,
profitably, within your resource capabilities. You know there is
an opportunity for successfully introducing a better mousetrap, and you have identified a target segment with needs that
can be met by your invention.

You must now develop your tactics for successfully implementing these strategic decisions. How *should* you plan and
carry out your marketing in today's competitive arena? In
brief, what are the tactics by which you can best deliver your
mousetrap to the target market?

We'll try to answer this question in some detail in this chapter. In doing so, we will focus on tactics for designing products and services to meet customers' needs, communicating their benefits effectively, and delivering them cost efficiently in a timely manner. At the same time, we will discuss securing feedback that will help you modify and shape your efforts through appropriate midcourse corrections. Before doing so, however, we will describe a tactical approach quite different from that dictated by the MBS approach.

A STRAW MAN

One approach — not the one we advocate, but a very common practice that bears examination — is to place the tactical burdens of marketing on account executives. Following this procedure, you select and train knowledgeable representatives, give them a list of prospective customers, and provide attractive mousetrap models or promotional brochures for use with prospects. You set sales quotas and reward the sales reps according to their diligence and success.

In other words, you attempt to overcome the inherent passivity of product-driven marketing tactics by switching to a sales-driven orientation. Rather than wait for customers to beat a path to your door, you become proactive, sending salespeople to call on potential customers and introduce them to your mousetraps (or your PBXs or energy-efficient motors or advertising services) and their advantages. The computer industry offers a classic example of product- and sales-driven approaches: Sun Microsystems builds terrific workstations and waits for customers to come to them; IBM builds good products and then merchandises and sells them aggressively. Becoming sales driven represents an important advance over the product-driven "mousetrap" sales effort (or lack thereof). It recognizes that a superior product or service is not enough to guarantee success in the marketplace.

According to mythology, if not in fact, such sales-driven, show-the-flag marketing was very successful in earlier days for organizations such as NCR and IBM. But that was during an era when prospects were not courted by so many strong competitors. Moreover, key decision makers were not so likely as they are today to be part of a complex organization and, as consequence, to be influenced by multiple constituencies. Furthermore, your customers were not so likely as they are today to expect their suppliers and service providers to recognize their needs and to be customer driven.

In fact, some account executives are effective and successful with sales-driven tactics, often by also focusing on such things as trust and reliability. But the flaw is in believing that universally uniform and aggressive selling can sell anybody anything anytime. One size rarely fits all. Selling on the basis of needs satisfaction is far more effective than by product "push." Can you afford to allow key tactical decisions to be made by the sales reps at the end of the pathway, without the active direction of decision makers involved in the overall planning and implementation effort? If you cannot, it is time to apply MBS lessons systematically in the design and implementation of marketing tactics.

AN OVERVIEW OF THE TACTICAL PLANNING EFFORT

What must be done next is to develop and implement the tactics that will turn strategic planning into reality. As important a role as direct selling plays in business-to-business marketing, it is only one of several channels for communicating with customers and delivering products and services. You regularly make additional choices about the use of direct selling and other distribution mechanisms, and you do so in the context of other tactical decisions. To do so in a manner consistent with MBS analysis and an MBS strategy, you want to develop those tactics as part of a carefully planned, customer-driven approach.

As you translate strategy into marketing success, planning and implementation include three key, interrelated steps. These steps are illustrated in Exhibit 29 and discussed below with a brief indication of the issues involved.

STEP 1: CREATE THE PRODUCT OR SERVICE AND SET ITS PRICING.

In the sales-driven approach, we implicitly assumed that the product and its price are fixed. But when and how did this occur? We may have identified our target market from a strategic point of view and focused on certain specific needs of this market that our manufacturing or service company can address. However, the design of the specific product or service and its key features remains to be specified, as does its pricing.

STEP 2: ESTABLISH TACTICS FOR THE POSITIONING OF THE PRODUCT OR SERVICE AND ITS IMPLEMENTATION THROUGH ADVERTISING, PROMOTION, SALES MATERIALS, AND SO ON.

In contrast to the account executive–centered sales-driven approach, we want our planning group to provide marketing representatives with guidance on the most effective positioning of products and services for the target market segments addressed. Moreover, we would want to consider the appropriate mix of advertising and promotional efforts.

141

Exhibit 29
STEPS IN NEEDS-BASED MARKETING

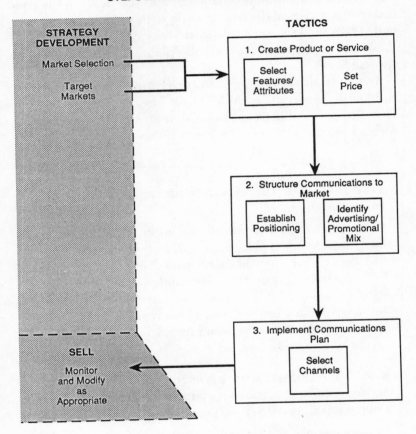

STEP 3: SELECT THE CHANNELS FOR INFORMATION DISTRIBUTION AND PRODUCT OR SERVICE SELLING.

Before investing major resources in advertising or in direct sales, we want to consider the relative value of different media, alone or in conjunction with other forms of communication. In addition, we should weigh the merits of reliance on corporate resources versus dependence on trade allies.

It must be pointed out that it may not be practical to follow these steps in exact sequence. For instance, channel selection (Step 3) may influence the creation of the product or service and its positioning.

In the following sections of this chapter, we will discuss each of these steps in greater detail and focus on their particular contributions to the implementation of needs-based marketing strategies. We will separate these tactical elements for clarity of presentation. However, we believe that the entire process must be integrated, with decisions at each step supporting and informing one another. For this reason, we will later return to a discussion of the overall tactical effort, to illustrate the importance of considering connections among the decisions. Finally, we will discuss the systematic collection of feedback for use in shaping and enhancing both the strategy and the tactics chosen.

CREATING THE PRODUCT OR SERVICE

You know the basic product or service you intend to market and the target group most appropriate to your strategic plan. To turn your plan into reality, you must now determine what specific features should be included in your PBX, your energy-efficient lighting program, or your accounting service, as well as what pricing structure should be applied.

PRODUCT AND SERVICE DESIGN TACTICS

Suppose your strategic analysis has led you to develop a software sales and consulting service targeted at restaurants and lounges. Having carefully analyzed the needs of the overall market and the current support systems for the food-and-beverage industry, you have discovered a niche that is open to your skills and resources. You are ready to offer your clients systems appropriate to their size that will handle ordering and inventory, sales, payroll, and tax issues in an integrated fashion. Your experience in the industry, coupled with your education and training with computers, has prepared you to tailor solutions to the specific needs of different sizes and types of restaurants and to construct custom programs, as well as projections of weekly and seasonal demand variations. What must you do at the tactical level?

To bring your software and consulting service to market, you must decide which attributes and features you will bundle into the basic package, which you will offer as an option, and which you will not provide. For example, will your service be limited to IBM and IBM-clone hardware, or will it include Apple Macintosh systems? Will you provide your clients with a soup-to-nuts, one-stop service, including consultation on hardware selection, maintenance, and training, or just package software?

Your answers to questions of this sort will define, at the tactical level, the product or service you are providing and the niche you are addressing. Moreover, your decisions are likely to determine the viability of your marketing and the success of your enterprise. A wrong choice can easily lead to failure with a major market segment or leave the door open for a competitor to better reach an unserved group of customers.

No one can guarantee that you will make the correct decisions and select the ideal features for success in the market you have targeted. However, use of the needs-based approach is more likely to yield useful directions than any other system we have studied.

Your benchmark MBS survey has provided critical information about the needs of different segments in your market. Furthermore, these data have helped you to identify potentially valuable attributes and features of your product or service. But you have probably found that your prospective customers are interested in many more characteristics than you can economically or profitably offer. Rather than providing all the components that could be desired, you must select those most likely to elicit purchase of your product or service.

At this point, you might consider selecting the features that are easiest or cheapest to include or most often mentioned as desirable by customers. Or you might test market one or more versions of your product or service. All of these selection methods have some virtue. However, none allows you to compare the differential market appeal of fully described products or services at a relatively modest cost.

To appreciate the problem before us, let's examine these approaches in detail for a moment. First, the selection of features on the basis of cost or ease of production omits the customer perspective altogether. Second, focusing on customers' reactions to individual product or service characteristics fails to provide information regarding the *combinations* of attributes that are important to prospects. For example, your restaurant industry software consultation service may not require maintenance arrangements when considered on its own merits; however, its inclusion may be crucial to success if you also provide consultation about hardware. Finally, test marketing is likely to be extremely expensive — particularly if you were to consider testing not one configuration, but alternative configurations.

As we indicated in Chapter 5, we believe that the most effective and cost-efficient procedure for development of product and service design tactics is to apply conjoint analysis to prospective customers. In brief, conjoint analysis consists of a three-step procedure for determining the values prospective customers place on different attributes and features of your product or service as part of the complete package comprising the product or service, as outlined in Exhibit 30.

If your strategic analysis has indicated that only one significant market segment offers your company opportunities for entry, you may not wish to go beyond a gross analysis of your prospective customers' values for attributes and features. However, the needs-based approach offers the freedom to conduct a much finer-grained analysis of your opportunities. After all, the different attributes and features being considered for inclusion in your product or service are likely to satisfy a diversity of customer needs and offer disparate benefits. Consequently, the various attributes and features will differ in their appeal to the needs-based segments found in your market.

For this reason, we recommend that you couple conjoint analysis with a needs-based survey. In other words, we believe that product and service development should include careful exploration of the opportunities for marketing different packages to different segments. First, specify the most attractive package for each segment you wish to serve. Second, identify the areas of overlap and difference, and the costs or other barriers to marketing multiple products and services. Third, select and develop the mix that best fits your strategy, capabilities, and tactical objectives.

This approach may seem somewhat odd in the abstract, but you will readily recognize it as being at the heart of the strategy that General Motors used so successfully for so many years in marketing Chevrolet, Pontiac, Buick, Oldsmobile,

Exhibit 30
THE PROCESS OF CONJOINT
ANALYSIS

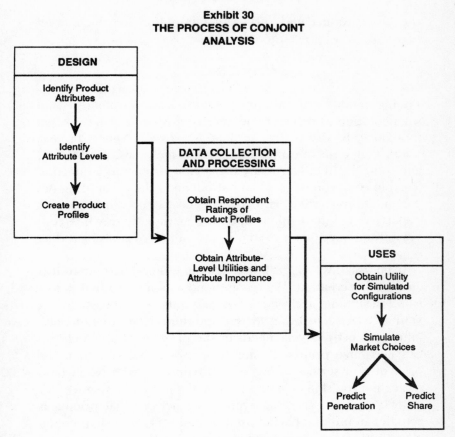

and Cadillac. Different customers are willing to make different trade-offs among attributes because they have different constellations of needs, as seen in needs-based analysis. By developing different bundles of attributes and features, you can appeal effectively to multiple segments. The keys to the successful development of product mix lies in understanding the needs of the different segments and the different trade-offs they are willing to make. This will allow you to construct

147

the best product and service configuration for the market segments you have targeted.

PRICING

Pricing should be just as sensitive to the lessons of needs-based segmentation as product and service design. Pricing is often thought to be driven by the need for responsiveness to your underlying costs of capital equipment, materials, production, and so forth. In effect, many firms view pricing as an uncomfortable compromise worked out between the accounting department, concerned with covering costs, and the marketing department, intent upon capturing market share while conveying an image of, for example, a premium or a basic product or service.

In contrast, we suggest pricing as an integral part of product and service creation. We recommend an approach that differs from designing a preferred configuration — uncosted — of your software consulting service and then attempting to ascertain your cost-recovery needs or the price point at which you can maximize profits. Rather we suggest that you treat the price of your service as one of its attributes, just as you would treat the provision or nonprovision of a particular feature like an 800 number. In other words, we believe that pricing is actually an integral part of product and service design, not an after-the-fact labeling of its value.

A major virtue of this approach is that critical information needed for pricing is readily available as part of the same needs-based survey work utilizing conjoint analysis suggested earlier. In brief, potential customers would be asked to trade off pricing attributes against other product or service attributes. This provides the relative preferences for lower prices or broader services, for example, that you require to design appropriate offerings. Moreover, it would allow you to consider a number of different pricing mechanisms in a coherent and systematic fashion. To illustrate, the conjoint analysis would permit you to determine whether customers prefer discounts in the form of lower list prices, rebates, low-interest loans, longer warranties, increased support service, or additional product or service features.

Finally, the use of needs-based segmentation information with the conjoint analyses would allow you to consider the development of differently priced packages for different customer segments. For example, you might expect that pricing a new PBX product low would make it more attractive to members of segments that are budget conscious than to those that are quality oriented or interested in multifeature compatibility.

Similarly, many electric utilities have been unable to decide whether to offer rebates or low-interest loans, or to engage in lease-purchase arrangements with their customers in their quest to promote customers' investment in more efficient equipment, such as commercial-sized chillers, as a means of reducing summer power needs. The MBS approach can indicate which customer segments are likely to prefer lease-purchase agreements, which are seeking to achieve or maintain liquidity, and so forth. Armed with this information, electric utilities can develop the appropriate mix of financial incentives to maximize the appeal of new equipment purchases among their customers.

ESTABLISHING THE PRODUCT OR SERVICE'S POSITIONING

Now that you have created the complete package of attributes and features of your product or service, including its pricing, you must determine how you will communicate its contents and the benefits it can provide your target markets. As we indicated earlier in this chapter, we'll focus on two aspects of tactical communications planning here, the development of your positioning and your selection of media.

POSITIONING

The objective of positioning is to create a preference for a product in the minds of potential buyers. As Al Ries and Jack Trout describe it in *Positioning: The Battle for Your Mind*, "Positioning is an organized system for finding a window in the mind [of a prospect]" (p. 19). The basic premise of positioning is that reality does not add up to sales. In other words, you can have an objectively superior product and still lose share because the competition created a perception that their product is better.

In the highly competitive arena of the 1990s, customers will be bombarded with messages designed to create preference for products and brands. To rise above the noise in this environment, you must find an open window in the mind of the prospect. As consumer product strategists have discovered, the way to reach the prospect is to create simple messages that connect with a need that already exists in the mind of the buyer. Competitive positioning messages touch the need in the prospect's mind while at the same time addressing competitors' positions, either directly or indirectly. One classic example of such a positioning in the consumer market is the "Uncola" message created by 7-Up.

Establishing competitive positionings in the business-to-business market is complicated by the presence of multiple buying influences. In the absence of information about the needs of the multiple influencers, strategists are left to design positioning messages that address only the needs of the target functional buyer. The Novell advertisement in *Business Week* that we cited in Chapter 3 is a classic example of a misplaced positioning caused by a lack of consideration of the needs that the target reader — senior executives — are likely to have. As you may recall, the Novell message focused on the technical features of a local area network management product. However, the audience of *Business Week* consists largely of business executives who are unlikely to be receptive to messages about the technical features of a product. A more effective positioning message for placement in *Business Week* might have mentioned that use of the Novell package will improve business productivity and reduce operating costs.

Because the MBS framework allows you to identify the needs of organizations and the needs of the major sources of influence on purchases, it is ideally suited to support the development of multitiered positionings. The advantage of multitiered positioning is that it gives you the ability to create messages that not only recognize common needs but also the distinct needs of individual target segments and key influencers within target segments. Exhibit 31 illustrates at least three tiers of positioning on the right, with segment profiles on the left. At the broadest level, there is a general positioning that is designed to appeal to needs that are shared by your target segments. A second, more focused tier of positioning messages recognizes the distinct needs of each target segment. The third tier of positioning messages reflects the separate needs of key influencers within each of the target segments.

In the following sections, we describe how you can use the MBS framework to establish this multitiered positioning.

THE FIRST TIER: USING MBS TO DEVELOP A GENERAL COMPETITIVE MESSAGE

An effective general competitive positioning message addresses one or more important needs that are shared by

Exhibit 31
MULTITIER POSITIONING

NEEDS ASSESSMENT	SEGMENT					
	1	2	3	4	5	6
Strategy Needs						
– Quality focus	●	○	●	○	●	○
– Price-competitive	○	●	●	○	●	○
– Accept risk	●	○	○	○	●	○
– Market responsiveness	●	○	○	●	●	●
– Innovation	●	○	●	○	●	○
– Communications as an asset	●	●	●	○	●	○
– Cost control	○	●	●	●	●	●
– Market expansion	●	●	●	○	●	○
Business Operations Needs						
– Grow skill base	●	○		○	○	●
– Increase productivity	●	●	●	○	●	○
– Improve performance quality	●	○	●	○	●	○
– Cross-functional integration	●	○	●	○	●	○
– Long-range planning	●	○	●	○	●	●
– Hierarchical control	●	●	○	○	●	●
– Improve communications	●	○	●	●	●	●
– Reduce operating costs	○	●	●	○	●	●
Telecommunications Needs						
– Standardization (open)	●	○	○	○	●	○
– Centralization (net. mgt.)	●	○	○	○	●	●
– Budget control	●	●	●	●	●	●
– Reduce vendor dependency	○	●	●	●	●	●
– Cost reduction	○	●	●	●	○	●
– Integration (voice/data)	●	○	●	○	●	○
Technology Needs						
– Reliability (error detection)	●	●	●	○	●	●
– Uptime (24 hours, 7 days/week)	●	○	●	○	●	○
– Security (high level)	●	○	○	○	○	○
– Service support (within 4 hours)	●	○	●	●	●	○
– User friendly (tracing)	●	●	○	●	●	●
– Compatible features	●	○	○	●	●	○

○ LOW ● HIGH

POSITIONING TIERS

TIER 1:

General Positioning Messages
- Communications as an asset
- Expand markets
- Increase productivity
- Extend budgetary controls
- Reliable products
- User friendly

TIER 2:

Target Segment (#2) Positioning Message
- Price-competitive markets
- Cost control
- Top-down control
- Reduce operating costs
- Reduce vendor dependency
- Reduce cost
- Fast response to service requests

TIER 3:

Senior Executive
- Price-competitive
- Communications an asset
- Cost control
- Market expansion
- Increase productivity
- Enables top-down control
- Reduce operating costs

Telecom Manager
- Budgetary control
- Reduce vendor dependency
- Reduce costs
- Service response
- User friendly
- Training

target segments that your product or service can satisfy but the competition cannot.

We have already seen in Chapter 3 that an electric utility might develop a common theme to address the needs of customer segments that have a high propensity to participate in a particular program. For example, to appeal to both Proactives and Dependents, the utility might position an air conditioner maintenance program to stress efficiencies, by citing long-term savings in operating costs, maximization of equipment efficiencies, and control of energy costs.

The development and use of this common theme should not obscure the fact that it offers certain benefits that are important to the first segment and not the second, as well as benefits that appeal to the second segment but not the first. Specifically, the emphasis on long-term cost savings recognizes the sensitivity to rates and energy-related investments of the Dependents, while the focus on operating equipment efficiencies addresses the needs of the Proactives. Nonetheless, while responding to the needs of both customer segments, the suggested positioning does so with a consistent, integrated theme.

The use of the MBS approach will not solve all your problems: For instance, while it provides general themes for creative use by your advertising or PR firm, it will not indicate the specific content or form of a successful advertising or promotional message. Creative development of your themes will continue to be a key element of success. But MBS will help guide you away from themes that alienate your target segments and away from internal contradictions as you tailor messages to multiple audiences.

The needs-based benchmark survey results (described

in Chapter 5) can be used to identify shared needs in six easy steps.

Step 1: List the needs of your target segments in order of importance.

Step 2: Identify needs that are important and shared by the target segments.

Step 3: List the needs satisfied by your product or service and by your competitors'.

Step 4: Compare the needs satisfied with the important and commonly shared target segment needs.

Step 5: Select the important, shared target needs for which your product or service is advantaged.

Step 6: Develop a positioning message that focuses on the common, shared needs and describes how your product or service satisfies these needs.

Exhibit 32 illustrates the stepwise development of a general competitive positioning message for a hypothetical PBX LAN product targeting Segments 3 and 5. Presumably, these target segments would have been chosen as targets based on an assessment of their attractiveness: the size of their expenditures or of the installed base of PBXs or multiplexers.

THE SECOND TIER: DEVELOPING SEGMENT-SPECIFIC POSITIONING MESSAGES

While you are developing the general competitive positioning message, you should also identify needs that are important yet distinct for each of your target segments in which your product or service is advantaged. These needs

Exhibit 32
EXAMPLE OF NEEDS-BASED POSITIONING

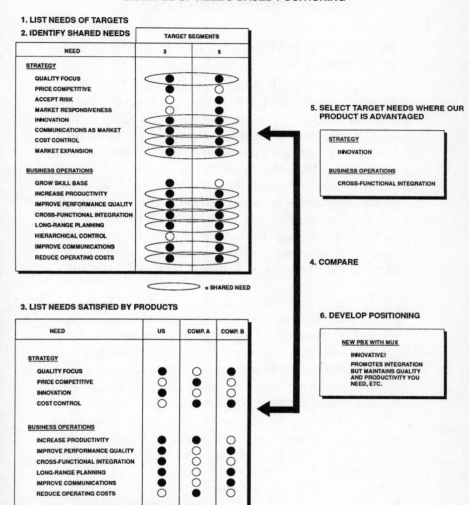

1. LIST NEEDS OF TARGETS
2. IDENTIFY SHARED NEEDS

NEED	TARGET SEGMENTS	
	3	5
STRATEGY		
QUALITY FOCUS	●	●
PRICE COMPETITIVE	●	○
ACCEPT RISK	○	●
MARKET RESPONSIVENESS	○	●
INNOVATION	●	●
COMMUNICATIONS AS MARKET	●	●
COST CONTROL	●	●
MARKET EXPANSION	●	●
BUSINESS OPERATIONS		
GROW SKILL BASE	●	○
INCREASE PRODUCTIVITY	●	●
IMPROVE PERFORMANCE QUALITY	●	●
CROSS-FUNCTIONAL INTEGRATION	●	●
LONG-RANGE PLANNING	●	●
HIERARCHICAL CONTROL	○	●
IMPROVE COMMUNICATIONS	●	●
REDUCE OPERATING COSTS	●	●

⬭ = SHARED NEED

5. SELECT TARGET NEEDS WHERE OUR PRODUCT IS ADVANTAGED

STRATEGY
  INNOVATION

BUSINESS OPERATIONS
  CROSS-FUNCTIONAL INTEGRATION

4. COMPARE

3. LIST NEEDS SATISFIED BY PRODUCTS

NEED	US	COMP. A	COMP. B
STRATEGY			
QUALITY FOCUS	●	○	●
PRICE COMPETITIVE	○	●	○
INNOVATION	●	○	○
COST CONTROL	○	●	●
BUSINESS OPERATIONS			
INCREASE PRODUCTIVITY	●	●	○
IMPROVE PERFORMANCE QUALITY	●	○	●
CROSS-FUNCTIONAL INTEGRATION	●	○	○
LONG-RANGE PLANNING	●	○	○
IMPROVE COMMUNICATIONS	●	○	●
REDUCE OPERATING COSTS	○	●	○

6. DEVELOP POSITIONING

NEW PBX WITH MUX

INNOVATIVE!
PROMOTES INTEGRATION
BUT MAINTAINS QUALITY
AND PRODUCTIVITY YOU
NEED, ETC.

155

will be used to design segment-specific positioning messages such as those illustrated in Exhibit 32.

THE THIRD TIER: DESIGNING KEY INFLUENCER POSITIONING MESSAGES

The concept of key influencer positioning accounts for the principles of business market purchase behavior we discussed in Chapter 3 — namely, that in the business market, the decision to acquire a product or service is frequently influenced by several levels within an organization, each attempting to satisfy needs that are relevant to their scope of responsibility. The objective of key influencer positioning is to develop separate positioning messages that reflect the key needs of each key influencer level within your target segments. Exhibit 34 presents an example of development of positioning messages designed to connect with the different needs of key influencer levels within a target segment.

As we have stressed throughout this book, buyers in the 1990s will be bombarded with positioning messages as they shop for customized products and services. The MBS framework will give you a decided competitive advantage in this environment. Because you can use the framework to customize the positioning message to fit the general needs of both the target business unit and the individual decision makers, your ability to sell them products and services that are perceived as meeting their needs will be enhanced. You will be better able to overcome the noise of competing messages, reach and touch the key decision makers, and establish awareness, interest, and preferences for your products and services in their minds.

MEDIA SELECTION TACTICS

Once you have developed your positioning messages, you will need to select your tactics for reaching the key decision makers in each targeted segment. Again, there is no magic bullet. No single mechanism can reach every decision maker or convey every message. Neither can one medium be identified as ideal for a given audience or a given message. Nonetheless, MBS provides tactical guidance for the effective and cost-efficient use of your resources and the application of information you have gathered through experience or systematic research.

Your key influencer positioning messages can be used in both general advertising and personal selling. The most critical concern is that the key influencer positioning message be used in media that reach the appropriate target key influencer audience. For example, in advertising, a positioning message focused on the cost-control needs expressed by senior managers in your target segments might be used in an advertisement in *Business Week*, while an advertisement highlighting the needs of functional-level key influencers might be placed in a trade magazine read by that audience.

Similarly, focused key influencer positionings can be used by sales personnel to connect more effectively with the needs of different decision makers they address. For instance, when a salesperson is talking to senior managers, the emphasis should be placed on meeting the senior management's strategy and operations needs. In contrast, when the salesperson is discussing the product or service with a target functional buyer, the positioning should be tailored to the needs of the functional buyer.

The basic tool in applying MBS to media selection is information about the appeal of different media to the key decision makers you have identified. Let us review three key guidelines you should consider.

GUIDELINE 1: CHOOSE A MEDIUM THAT IS LIKELY TO REACH THE TARGET.

Some decision makers prefer to read the trade or professional press in their field, while others prefer the general business press. Many people respond well both to personal contact and to direct mail, while others attend to one but not the other. The general tendencies of decision makers in different needs-based segments, illustrated in Exhibit 33, provide a framework for planning your media selection.

GUIDELINE 2: SELECT A MEDIUM THAT FITS WITH THE POSITIONING MESSAGE YOU WANT TO CONVEY.

Not every medium is appropriate for every message, whether because of editorial policies, technical limitations, or audience expectations. For example, you would not attempt to place a story about the engineering behind your new PBX with multiplexer in *Business Week*.

GUIDELINE 3: SPEND THE NECESSARY RESOURCES TO FOLLOW GUIDELINES 1 AND 2.

Many media are available today. Some are very specialized and reach only narrow audiences, while others are more general and have broad reach. Given the investment required to use virtually any medium, it is always tempting to select those with the greatest overall reach. However, the correct choice depends on your targets, their information needs, and your chosen positioning. The key to cost efficiency lies in focusing your resources on achieving impact rather than on reach itself. In addi-

Exhibit 33
PROMOTIONAL MEDIA AND
SELLING CHANNEL PREFERENCES

	Segment 1	Segment 2	Segment 3	Segment 4	Segment 5	Segment 6	Segment 7	Segment 8	Segment 9
Direct Contact	High	Low	Low	Low	Low	Low	High	Low	Low
Mail	Low	Medium	High	High	High	High	Low	High	High
Telephone	Low	Medium	Medium	Low	High	Low	Low	Low	Low
Newspapers	High	Medium	High	High	Low	High	Low	Low	High
Trade Literature	High	Medium	Low	Low	Low	High	High	Low	High

● High   ◐ Medium   ○ Low

tion to careful initial selection of media to reach *your* target efficiently, this translates into careful and constant monitoring of customers' awareness and acceptance of your message for continuing refinement of your promotional efforts.

In other words, you cannot concentrate only on the *number* of sales calls, the *volume* of direct mailings, or the *size* of the trade journal's subscription list. Rather, you must identify and implement measures of media and positioning effectiveness, whether they be telephone calls that follow up on marketing presentations or systematic reader surveys. These efforts require time and money, but they are essential to tuning your promotional strategy to the needs of your customers.

SELLING YOUR PRODUCT OR SERVICE

Thus far, you have used your strategic analysis to design the features of your product or service, including its price, and to develop the positioning you wish to create in the minds of your target segment or segments, as well to select the advertising and promotional media you will use to communicate with them. In this section, we will focus on the distribution system for getting your product or service to the target segment. Recognizing the problem of delivering your messages and products and services to the critical decision makers, however, we will begin with a brief discussion of the problem of reaching key members of the decision-making unit.

MULTIPLE ENTRY POINTS

In much of your marketing, sales, and delivery efforts, you must focus on specific decision makers within your target segments. As we have noted at several points, the major organizations to which we market are often complex. The MBS approach should sensitize you to the complexities of the multi-person DMU, as well as to the needs of the different buying units within a given company. For example, having identified schools as a market with major potential for your new heat pump, should you address members of the school board, the superintendent, the operating engineer, or teachers? Frankly, we doubt that there is a single answer that will apply in all cases. But what we do know is that each group is likely to have different needs (budget control, parental satisfaction with student comfort, ease of maintenance, and localized operational control). Consequently, you must be prepared to position and communicate the equipment's pertinent features and advantages to each constituency.

If you carefully survey the needs of your target segment, attending to the different levels of influencers, you should also understand key commonalities and incongruities among them. In some organizations, the business strategy needs of senior executives may translate directly into operational needs and functional needs. For example, we identify a company with a quality focus, willing to accept risk and seeking innovativeness, that also seeks to grow its skill base while increasing communication and improving performance quality. Furthermore, in building its telecommunications capabilities, this company seeks state-of-the-art network management and voice and data integration capabilities.

In such an atmosphere of congruity among the needs of the various decision makers, you have a major opportunity to market, for example, a new air-conditioning system by going in at the top and selling the senior executives on the equipment's strategic benefits. (You must also keep operational personnel aware of developments, to avoid creating resentments.) Indeed, if all levels of management are fully conversant with a consistent corporate strategy, you might even succeed through working with a key midlevel executive who can act as your guide to senior management needs and as your internal champion.

Unfortunately, such complete congruity appears all too infrequently. While we don't expect many successful organizations to show contradictory needs at different levels, we are likely to find that the needs of operational managers and those of senior executives may be quite distinct from one another and even that members of the buying center are unaware of the differences they bring to the group's decision making as a whole.

The role of the MBS approach is to help you recognize and

respond to the needs of the different influencers. By clarifying the needs of various decision makers, needs-based segmentation reinforces concern for careful assessment of the role and relative power of each member of the buying center. Moreover, MBS provides you with mechanisms for responding effectively to the pertinent needs of the key decision makers. Finally, the approach should sensitize you to the necessity of promoting your product or service to different members of a DMU.

Once again, a simple set of procedures facilitates tactical application of your knowledge. In essence, many of the tactics involved in creating and marketing your products and services at a general level are distilled into this process of focusing on a particular sales prospect (Exhibit 34).

Step 1: Identify the influencers of the purchase decision and their roles and responsibilities in your segments.

Step 2: Assess the needs of each of the key influencers, keeping in mind the needs dimension pertinent to each.

Step 3: Select the key influencers whose needs you can address through appropriate positioning.

Step 4: Develop a coordinated positioning message and select advertising and promotional channels appropriate to the pertinent decision makers.

DISTRIBUTION TACTICS

If your sales efforts have been successful to this point, your customer will be in direct contact with a representative or agent of your company. This contact may be in the form of sales calls, product delivery, or service calls, and it may be with your employee, a franchisee, or a trade ally. How should you structure this contact? For example, should you franchise the distribution network for your new air-conditioning system or run it internally?

As with all other aspects of the marketing mix, the selection of tactics is yours and should reflect your understanding of customer needs, your strengths and limitations, and your judg-

Exhibit 34
STEPS IN FOCUSING ON KEY INFLUENCERS

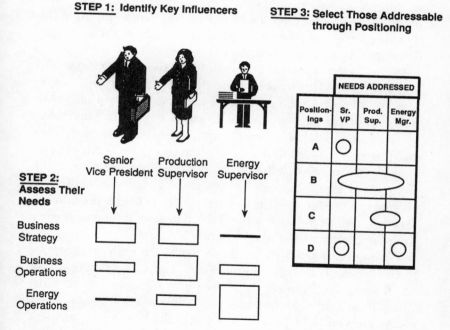

STEP 1: Identify Key Influencers

STEP 3: Select Those Addressable through Positioning

Senior Vice President   Production Supervisor   Energy Supervisor

STEP 2: Assess Their Needs

Business Strategy

Business Operations

Energy Operations

Position-ings	NEEDS ADDRESSED		
	Sr. VP	Prod. Sup.	Energy Mgr.
A	◯		
B		⬯	
C			⬯
D	◯		◯

STEP 4: Develop Coordinated Message and Delivery Options
• Assure consistent message in positionings A, B, C, D
• Select channels appropriate to positionings: e.g., A in *Business Week*

ments of who will be most effective in dealing with your customers.

In addressing these issues, you should consider both start-up and long-range factors. In the short run, you may be constrained to a large extent by your technical and financial ability, and the presence or absence of an independent infrastructure. For instance, you may not have the personnel available to service the new air-conditioning system you have developed and therefore may have to franchise out any maintenance or repair work. In the long run, however, you do have choices. You could plow some of your air conditioner profits into the training of an in-house service staff, or you could use the profit in other ways. Your decision as to the long-range design of the distribution system should be guided by customer information developed from your needs-based surveys.

Just as we have seen in other contexts, the keys to successful application of MBS tactics to the design of a distribution system lie in knowing the customer's needs and in your ability to match your product or service to those needs. In particular, you should recall that, when reviewing the business operations and functional needs that differentiate commercial customers, we saw that service delivery and relationships are prominent factors. For example, some customers seek internal control of all major functions, while others prefer reliance on outside services. Some indicate a need for constant interaction with their suppliers, while others do not.

We can further illustrate these issues through an example from the electric utility industry. A company serving a few small towns in a largely rural area may be forced to provide installation and maintenance for efficient commercial-sized chillers, given the lack of independent dealers and repair persons in the area. In the short run, should the service calls be made by electric utility personnel or by a contractor certified by the utility? In the long run, should the utility train and develop a group of independent contractors? Since relationships with utility representatives are critical to one of the segments targeted, we would expect a program using in-house utility personnel to be considerably more successful than one based on contract or certified outsiders.

The following six simple steps, illustrated in Exhibit 35, describe the development and refinement of the most appropriate system for distributing your product or service to your target segment.

Step 1: List the points of contact between your company and your target segment, such as person-to-person sales, delivery, installation, telephone support, and service.

Step 2: Identify the needs of your target segments that may be affected by the delivery system at each of those contact points.

Step 3: Specify the delivery agents available to you for serving customers at each of the contact points.

Step 4: Assess the strengths and weaknesses of each delivery agent with respect to satisfying the customer needs you have identified. (Of course, the economics associated with each agent must be considered here as well.)

Step 5: Match the most effective delivery agents for each customer segment to the contact points they can support.

Step 6: If the most effective delivery agents are not currently available or are not financially viable, formulate a plan for developing them.

This approach is applicable to all aspects of the distribution system, including the selection of wholesalers and franchisees, as well as trade allies in general.

Exhibit 35
OPTIMIZING THE DISTRIBUTION SYSTEM

ANALYSIS

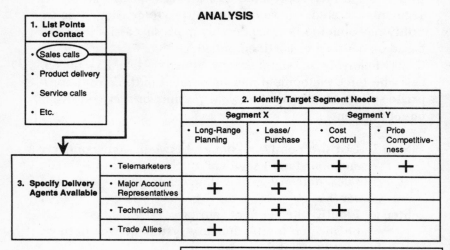

		2. Identify Target Segment Needs			
		Segment X		**Segment Y**	
		• Long-Range Planning	• Lease/ Purchase	• Cost Control	• Price Competitive- ness
3. Specify Delivery Agents Available	• Telemarketers		+	+	+
	• Major Account Representatives	+	+		
	• Technicians		+	+	
	• Trade Allies	+			

1. List Points of Contact
- (Sales calls)
- Product delivery
- Service calls
- Etc.

4. Assess Strengths/Weaknesses of Delivery Agents in Meeting Needs

SELECTION/ENHANCEMENT

5. Match Agents to Segments

6. Develop Current or Additional Agents to Address Unmet Needs

Segment

	X	Y
Telemarketers		+
Major Account Representatives	+	

166

INTEGRATING YOUR TACTICAL EFFORTS

For ease of presentation, we have spent most of this chapter discussing marketing tactics in terms of discrete components, such as product and service design, pricing, positioning, and delivery. Moreover, we have treated these components in a linear fashion, as if they can be unequivocally arrayed along a time line, from the creation of a product or service through communication with customers to ultimate delivery. We recognize, however, that this is an oversimplification of the real-world problems of marketing. In this section, we will consider briefly the interdependencies of different marketing tactics, and, in the final section of this chapter, we will discuss the need for tracking and monitoring our marketing efforts.

Our point is quite simple. Not only will MBS provide important direct value as you create your marketing tactics, but it will also yield indirect benefits through its effects on your corporate marketing culture.

To be sure you have developed the best product or service possible and positioned it most effectively to meet the needs and preferences of your target segments, you should continually review your entire package as you create and implement the marketing mix. Check, for example, that the distribution system you have designed meets the needs of the same segments as do the other features and attributes of your product or service. Be sure, as well, that your selection of advertising and promotional tactics is consistent with the pricing you have matched to your customers' needs. It may be extremely useful to supplement your own analysis of these issues through qualitative interviews (focus groups) with members of your target segments, or even through quantitative surveys assessing reactions to the total product and service package among those customers.

You already know the importance of having all departments that affect your marketing success work from the same playbook. Unless product development is sensitive to customer needs, the task of the advertising department is Herculean: Throughout this book, we have stressed the fact that products and services do not sell themselves — they must fill customers' needs. Unless those who price your products and services work with product development, the cost structures that emerge may satisfy neither your customers nor your corporate hierarchy.

Beyond its other qualities, needs-based MBS provides an understanding of customers' needs and a vision of how to reach them that is consistent and communicable. In other words, MBS helps tacticians in every department identify and work with the same analytic structure. By this relatively simple mechanism, you can enhance communication among internal departments and ensure the consistency of your company's marketing program.

SYSTEMATIC ASSESSMENT OF CUSTOMER FEEDBACK

Indeed, you can achieve major advances in becoming a customer-driven marketer through routine, systematic tracking and monitoring of your customers' reactions to the products and services you offer.

An initial benchmark survey provides an important key to the successful creation, positioning, and delivery of your products and services. But it is not a prescription for instant success: The translation of insights from the needs-based information to the marketing mix includes some art and carries many uncertainties. Moreover, customers are likely to change over time, as their economic situation changes and their own customers shift. Finally, competitors are also likely to shift in their composition and their thrust. For all these reasons, your benchmark data will eventually grow stale. As we have emphasized previously, unless you track and monitor customers' needs and the effectiveness of your marketing tactics, share may be lost to your competitors.

In this dynamic marketing arena of the 1990s, you cannot afford failing to track and monitor customers' needs and their satisfaction with your products and services. It is likely that you already track the quality of your products and services and the effectiveness of your advertising and promotions, as well as your sales force. You probably collect much of this information from internal records, your advertising agency, trade allies, and sales force. But you must also continue to involve customers beyond the initial needs-based survey; you must regularly check the degree to which they believe your products and services are meeting their needs.

The need for continuous tracking and monitoring imposes two corollary requirements to become a fully market-driven company. First, you must develop a refined data collection system, as well as the capability of analyzing, interpreting, and applying those data. Second, you must create a sophisticated management information system that will allow you to access, compare, and integrate the data from different surveys and sources of information.

In these last several chapters, we have already set forth the key requirements of the data collection system and relevant application issues. The management information system issues will be addressed in the next chapter.

7

MARKET-DRIVEN CUSTOMER INFORMATION SYSTEMS

Most companies have failed to build effective systems for accessing information about their customers. Often, they have market research systems that report results from individual primary research (like product tests) or from single secondary data sources (like market audits), but there is usually no linkage across research data sources or to other types of data sources such as billing or sales. Certainly, companies have billing systems containing little more than names, addresses, and phone numbers in addition to amounts billed and shipment or sales data. But from a marketer's point of view, even when billing and shipment data are linked, this information is very limited: It does not tell us much about customers, and what it does tell us covers only present (and not potential) customers. What is needed is an overarching system for integrating multiple sources of information about customers: a Customer Information System (CIS).

A comprehensive CIS can be costly to create and maintain, and that is probably the main reason why companies do not have them. A CIS can, after all, entail a substantial investment in an overhead support function. On the other hand, we have urged you to become more market driven, illustrating the benefits of letting your actions be dictated by the needs and wants of your customers. By committing to that perspective, you have already placed a premium on customer information, so ready access to it via a CIS should have a high value to you.

In this chapter, we will reinforce that value by presenting the benefits of a market-driven CIS, one in which customer needs and the needs-based framework are important components. We will also discuss some of the properties of a market-driven CIS that will best support your program's marketing objectives. And we will discuss some of the steps you can take to facilitate the effective creation and integration of such a system. It should be noted that this is not a systems designer's handbook: We will not give details on data collection, system architecture, software design, or hardware selection. Rather, we will focus on managerial issues: How you, as a manager, can benefit from such a system, what some of its desirable features are, and what you can do to facilitate implementation.

WHAT ARE THE BENEFITS OF A MARKET-DRIVEN CUSTOMER INFORMATION SYSTEM?

A Customer Information System is a system that allows the storage, retrieval, analysis, and display of customer data. Because the amount and complexity of such data are usually great and because the analysis and display needs are more than rudimentary, it is a given that such systems are computerized.

A Market-driven Customer Information System (M-CIS) is one in which customer needs are a central component (Exhibit 36). Our premise is that understanding needs is essential to effective marketing, and our distinction of an M-CIS from a plain CIS merely emphasizes this point. Many of the points we will cover in this chapter relate as much to plain CISs as to M-CISs, so there is no need to dwell on the distinction between the two.

Nonetheless, we maintain the distinction for a good reason, illustrated in Exhibit 36: to remind you that the primary purpose of a CIS is to allow you to relate customer needs to other characteristics so that you can maximize the use of needs data in your marketing decisions. The MBS framework is a powerful one, but being able to translate it into action is important. Identifying the media-viewing patterns of decision makers in a

Exhibit 36
THE NEED FOR A MARKET-DRIVEN CIS

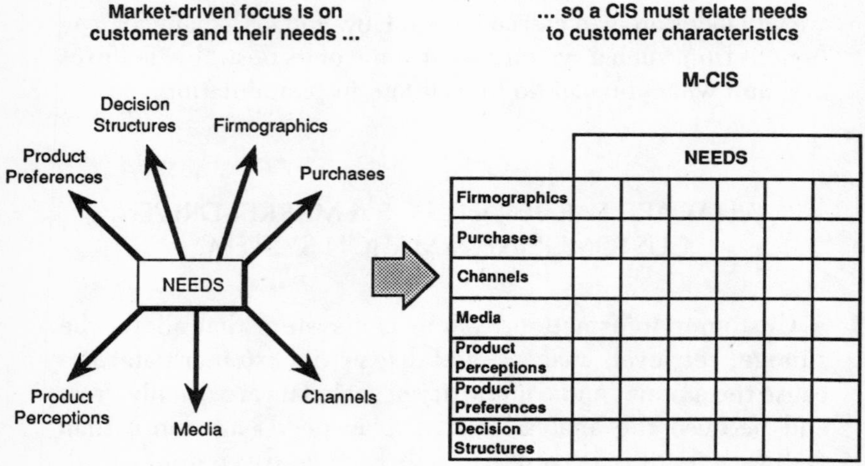

172

particular needs segment, for instance, allows more efficient ability to reach the members of that segment with advertising. If properly constructed and used, an M-CIS will be a powerful tool for integrating MBS into your corporate culture by making it accessible to everyone.

An ideal M-CIS contains many different types of customer information from a variety of data sources. In addition to the critically important customer needs, useful data types may include:

- firmographics (e.g., location, industry, employee size, financial data), measures of success or dominance in their markets, organizational structure, and variables related to volume, such as square footage for HVAC systems, number of end-points for computer networks, and number of franchises for fast-food chains
- the nature of your customers' businesses: the wants and needs of *their* customers (which in turn influence your customers' decisions) and your customers' competitive status and market success
- product-purchase history for you or your competitors, brand switching, billing history, products currently owned or leased, volume or frequency of product or service used, plans for future purchases
- current profitability for you (based on revenues produced minus your cost to provide the product or service) and potential profitability for you (requiring an ability to estimate the potential size of purchase or usage and to subtract out the cost of providing)
- any pertinent constraining factors, such as compatibility with current equipment
- decision-making structure, including the roles of key influencers

- distribution channel usage — which ones and how much
- media-viewing patterns
- product perceptions and preferences — performance perceptions, likes and dislikes, attitudes and beliefs about your products and those of your competitors, feature preferences, and needs

It is not unusual for a company to have much of these data available in a variety of disparate formats. The role of a good M-CIS is to integrate as many of the customer databases as possible into a single system so that use of the information can be optimized.

Note that we did not include payroll accounting systems, inventory systems, general economic environment data information on current technology developments and trends, regulatory data, and the like in the above list. None of these is customer data and so does not fit in with a narrow definition of a Customer Information System. This exclusion is not meant to imply that we consider such information to be immaterial; for example, relating customer needs to technology trends may be a useful way to aid product development resource allocation. Generally, however, those noncustomer data sources are analyzed separately and independently of customer data because they have entirely different uses. The incorporation of an M-CIS into a larger management information system is a more general problem that will not be treated here.

An effective M-CIS is an important part of your corporate infrastructure supporting planning, selling, market research, and monitoring functions. The most important function of an M-CIS is to support *planning* in many parts of your organization: marketing, product development, and sales. Chapters 5 and 6 provided our view of the kinds of information needed both for strategic and tactical planning, with particular emphasis on the market structure analysis. The M-CIS provides the basic information needed in analyzing market and product opportunities, portfolio value analyses, and selection of markets and target segments. The M-CIS should also assist you in product feature optimization, in pricing, positioning, and promotion executions, and in distribution channel selection, as illustrated in Chapter 6. Exhibits 22 to 26 in Chapter 5 and Exhibits 32 to 35 in Chapter 6 provide illustrations of the kinds of information that would be useful in many different phases of planning.

An M-CIS should support *selling* by identifying the needs and other characteristics of current or prospective customers and of the organizations they belong to. To be effective, salespeople must know what to say to their customers. In direct sales, where selling is carried out on a one-to-one basis, an M-CIS can be a potent tool if it contains individual customer information as in Exhibit 37. By highlighting needs or other characteristics on which the customer and the customer's organization is unusual, the sales rep can focus on the important aspects in dealing with the customer.

Your sales rep may also find it beneficial to share any information you have on your customers' markets with them. For instance, a manufacturer of beverages sold through retail outlets often knows a great deal about the needs and wants of consumers of the beverage category. The manufacturer would probably benefit greatly from sharing that information with the retailer: Besides being of direct assistance to the retailer in selling the manufacturer's product, it also conveys an attitude of cooperation that retailers will greatly appreciate.

The use of an M-CIS in the context of the MBS framework also allows ready identification of key elements missing from

Exhibit 37
AN M-CIS CUSTOMER PROFILE—SIMPLE EXAMPLE

Customer: _____

Address: _____

Dept.: _____ Div.: _____ Co.: _____

SIC Codes: _____ No. of Employees: _____ FY Total Revenues: _____

Decision Matrix

KEY INFLUENCERS		ROLES			
Name	Position	Recomm	Evaluate	Choose	Veto
___	___	___	___	___	___
___	___	___	___	___	___
___	___	___	___	___	___
___	___	___	___	___	___
___	___	___	___	___	___

Selling Channel Preference

CHANNEL

Direct _____

Mail/Phone _____

3rd Party _____

Equipment

	Total FY Expenditures	FY Expenditures on Us	Vendor	No. of Units
PBX	_____		_____	_____
Multiplexer	_____	_____	_____	_____
Modems	_____	_____	_____	_____

Needs

	SCORE
STRATEGIC	
• Quality	_____
• Price	_____
• Innovation	_____
OPERATIONS	
• Grow Skill Base	_____
• Increase Productivity	_____
• Improve Performance	_____
TELECOM MANAGEMENT	
• Standardize	_____
• Centralize	_____
• Cost Control	_____

Needs Segment:
_____

the customer profile, providing focus for the sales rep on the most important elements for further exploration with the customer. And it would be extremely helpful if the M-CIS could prioritize the sales rep's customers (current or potential) in terms of potential attractiveness.

Market research is an area that can benefit from a comprehensive M-CIS. Identification of the most relevant populations for product testing and for market audits is greatly facilitated if much is known about current and potential customers. Similarly, the most revealing areas for test marketing of new products can be identified if you know which kinds of customers are most critical to product success and how those customers can be reached (Exhibit 38).

Once strategies have been implemented, products tested and introduced, and customers contacted, the job of the M-CIS does not stop. It must also perform a *monitoring* function (Exhibit 39). Evaluation of the performance of your marketing and sales activities against plans is critical, and the kinds of data already tracked in the M-CIS are central to that evaluation. Analysis of your competitors' activities on an ongoing basis is also more than an incidental function of the M-CIS. A good M-CIS not only provides you with sales figures, but the ability to diagnose causes: why things are going well and where there are problems. Such diagnostics may be critical to your ability to react quickly and fix problems before they become disasters.

One benefit of an M-CIS that is less tangible, but nonetheless important, is its durability. In our business world, in which promotions, reorganizations, and job churning are inevitable, companies often suffer a kind of corporate amnesia in which much that is learned by an individual in a function is lost when the individual leaves that function. It is important for some element of your company to represent a force for continuity, and information systems often perform some of that

Exhibit 38
USING M-CIS TO SELECT TEST MARKET FOR A NEW PRODUCT

		NEEDS-BASED SEGMENTS (Targets Circled)				
	1	(2)	3	(4)	(5)	6
Existing Product Shares						
Us	50	30	30	20	10	50
Competitor A	30	40	30	50	30	10
Competitor B	10	20	30	10	40	10
Other	10	10	10	20	20	30
Projected Attractiveness of New Product	Weak	Strong	Moderate	Strong	Strong	Weak
Total Expenditures in Category	$10MM	$20MM	$5MM	$15MM	$20MM	$5MM
Geographic Distribution						
North	●	○	●	○	○	●
South	○	●	○	●	○	●
East	○	○	○	●	○	●
West	○	●	●	●	●	○
Size of Account						
Small	○	○	●	○	○	●
Medium	●	○	○	○	●	○
Large	○	●	○	●	●	○
Channel Usage						
Direct	○	●	○	○	●	○
Mail/phone	●	○	●	○	○	●
Third party	●	○	○	●	○	○

Selected Test Market: Large, Western accounts
using direct selling and third-party
allies selling to those large accounts

178

Exhibit 39
MONITORING PERFORMANCE

TOTAL MARKET

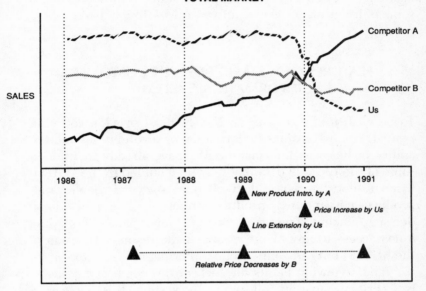

PERFORMANCE BY SEGMENT

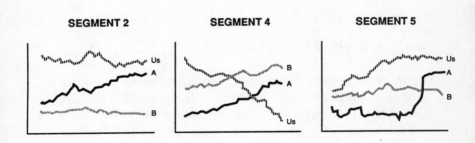

179

function. Systems tend to outlast individuals. When an employee leaves a position, all the valuable information about customers stored in his or her head is not completely lost if some of it has made its way into your M-CIS database.

FEATURES OF A MARKET-DRIVEN CUSTOMER INFORMATION SYSTEM

To be most useful to you, an M-CIS must provide you with ready access to customer information of several types and the ability to link this information. We have already mentioned some of the types of data that may be included in the system: firmographics, purchase data, channel usage, media viewing, product perceptions, product preferences, organizational decision-making structures, and customer needs. Providing quick access to any of these data is the primary function of the M-CIS, but the ability to link information — for example, the media-viewing habits for each of the needs segments — is *the* critical capability offered by the system. It is this feature that provides the data illustrated in every example in this and the last two chapters showing results supporting planning, sales, research, and monitoring.

THE SINGLE CUSTOMER RECORD CONCEPT

In order to provide this linking capability, the M-CIS must be structured logically, as illustrated in Exhibit 40. The M-CIS database must organize customer data *by customer*. You can think of data for a given customer as being combined into a huge, single record, with a location on the record for every

Exhibit 40
CONCEPTUAL LAYOUT FOR PARTS
OF AN M-CIS CUSTOMER RECORD

	Customer	Address	...	Media Viewing	...	Decision Matrix	...
Location Number	1	2	...	15	...	38 – 65	...

		Equipment Stock	...		Strategic Needs	Operations Needs	...
Location Number	...	103 – 217		...	329 – 340	341 – 348	...

		Telecommunication Management Needs	Segment Membership	...
Location Number	...	349 – 363	364	...

possible item of information. With this layout, it is easy to construct the kinds of links that we need. For example, examination of media-viewing habits by needs segment amounts to little more than counting the number of customers in each segment who view each identified medium. So long as both needs segment membership and media-viewing behavior are recorded on the logical data record for customers, such a link is possible.

If the customer record is not laid out in this form — if it does not at least conceptually contain both media-viewing and needs segment data — it is nearly impossible to get a valid estimate of media viewing by segment. Obviously, this concept extends to any other comparison or relationship you wish to examine in the customer data. The customer-record layout also facilitates the profiling of individual customers that is so useful in direct selling. If we wish to know the characteristics that distinguish a customer in order to better meet that customer's needs, it is much easier to do if all information is together in a single record than if several different data sources must be consulted.

It is not really necessary that the actual records in the M-CIS be laid out as shown in Exhibit 40. In fact, it would rarely be efficient to create such an immense single record for each customer. If media-viewing and segment membership data are contained in separate files, the comparison between the two can still be made if corresponding records for the same customer can be identified and assembled. The technology for accomplishing this is called *relational database management* and is widely available in a number of software packages. In essence, a single partial data record for the customer, containing only the information needed, is assembled on the fly from different databases. Unfortunately, information systems often contain a number of databases, created and maintained independently, with no easy way to link the records of a single customer. There may well be efficiencies in maintaining separate databases, but the system must be designed via relational database management so that it behaves, at least conceptually, as shown in Exhibit 40. The single logical customer record is an important property of an effective M-CIS.

CURRENT AND POTENTIAL CUSTOMERS

Being responsive to customer needs means more than attending to your own customers. If you are to expand your business and develop a reputation for being a quality provider of goods or services, you must also keep your eye on people who are not currently using your product but are potential buyers.

It is natural to be concerned about keeping your current customers happy, but significant growth in your business will most likely come from new customers or new markets for your products, not from selling more to your current customers. If the information system that supports your planning does not take into account the needs and other characteristics of non-customers, you may be missing important opportunities.

ACCOMMODATING CHANGE IN THE SYSTEM

Typically, the customer record has some holes in it — some customers have not been assigned to needs segments, for example. For others, we may not have complete data on their purchase of competitors' products. For some, we may not even know simple firmographic information, such as number of employees. And, in general, any item of information can be out of date if the data have not been refreshed recently.

Ideally, we will be continually filling these holes. An M-CIS must be a dynamic system that is continually changing and being updated. As you conduct more research and your sales reps gather more information, the system must facilitate adding those data to the customer records. Furthermore, the database must be easily expanded when it becomes apparent that a new type of data would be important to track. For instance, if you have never kept needs data in your customer records, it would be a shame if your information system made it difficult to add these data. And conventions must be developed for deleting information when it becomes out of date.

As we become more sophisticated in our knowledge of our customers, it may become possible to fill holes in the database by imputing values based on other customer characteristics.

For example, we might create a model for predicting the potential profitability of a customer based on a number of characteristics, such as size, liquidity, and certain preferences for products with particular features. With such a model, we estimate profitability for any customer for whom we know the predicting characteristics, even customers who are not currently buyers of our products. This is a very cost-effective way of filling in holes in the database: by estimating values. However, it is important to distinguish real data from estimates in the database. Models are often imprecise in their predictions, and it is generally preferable to replace estimates with actual data whenever possible.

ACCESSIBILITY OF THE SYSTEM

Insist on a system that is easy for the analyst to use. This means that the user interface must be intuitively understandable, one that does not require significant training in order to use it effectively. We have seen some very sophisticated systems go unused because the analysts did not really understand how to get useful information from them. Likewise, the system should not require a great deal of retraining time. You will sometimes not use a system for weeks at a time. When you come back to it, the amount of effort necessary for relearning the system should be minimal.

Accessibility also means widespread availability of entry points to the system. In today's world, that means a microcomputer system, probably a network that can serve a large number of users from a single, common database. Most business environments have standardized on IBM PC systems and their close relatives; however, it must be pointed out that this is not the only successful option.

Accessibility also implies security issues. Who gets access to what information on the system? Many businesses have a need-to-know policy about sensitive information, and an M-CIS, with its many layers of data sources, can require careful planning for security. It is important, however, that those who need information not be discouraged from accessing it. Too many barriers negate the benefits of having the system in the first place.

Another very serious issue is the confidentiality of customers' data. Data are often collected with a direct or implied assurance of anonymity to the person supplying the data. This is particularly true of data that are collected in market research. Such confidentiality of customers' data should be respected if you value your customers. This means that the system must have the means of prohibiting access to certain types of data for some purposes. For example, it may not be possible for a sales rep to view a particular customer's needs data if the data were collected under a confidentiality agreement. On the other hand, it may be possible to view those same data *in the aggregate* for an entire industry class or for some other population of customers.

ANALYTIC CAPABILITIES

Access to all the information in the world will do you little good if you do not have an adequate means of analyzing it and reducing it to meaningful form. A good example of data overload occurred in the package goods industry when scanner systems were installed at the checkout lanes in grocery stores. For the first time, highly accurate data were available on all purchases at an incredible level of detail, including the date and time of each purchase. The sheer volume of data was enormous: Each purchased item's UPC code identified not only its brand, but the price for which it was actually purchased, the size of the container, and the flavor that it came in. To this day, the primary barrier to the usefulness of those data has been inability to simply and efficiently integrate, synthesize, and analyze it all.

The kinds of results you wish to use in your business decisions will dictate the analytic capabilities of your system. The possibilities range from simple sorting functions to complex statistical modeling to sophisticated graphics capabilities. We will not cover analytic methods in great detail here — we simply provide a synopsis of common methods as suggestive of some of the capabilities that you should find useful.

In general, the analytic techniques for conducting aggregated or mass analyses designed to identify, characterize, or monitor target populations are different from the more limited techniques used to analyze and profile individual customers.

The most common and most fundamentally useful tool in an information system is the simple cross-tabulation. Tables showing counts or averages on a customer characteristic for each of a group of customers are the most direct and easily understood method of representing a relationship between two items of information. A good M-CIS will allow you to easily "slice and dice" your database in any way that you see fit.

Trend analysis — the portrayal and forecasting of events over time — is another very common analytic technique for aggregate analyses. Everyone is familiar with sales figures over time, but the same techniques of analysis should apply to any item of data collected at a series of points in time. It should even be possible to track needs over time, although in our experience, needs change very slowly, without anything like the volatility of sales data. Forecasting trends into the future, based on performance in the past, is a very necessary part of planning a business, and tools should be readily available in your M-CIS for carrying out such analyses.

The ability to develop prediction models is also an important one when analyzing data in aggregate. Various forms of regression analysis and other kinds of predictive modeling techniques should be provided to allow the analyst free rein to explore relationships in the database. As an example, we mentioned above the possibility of predicting profitability from such characteristics as size, liquidity, and product feature preferences.

Furthermore, once such a model has been developed, the ability to exercise it is also important: "what if" analyses in which assumptions in the model are altered and the resulting changes in prediction are examined. For example, we might be able to predict that an expected reduction in liquidity due to worsening economic conditions might weaken the predicted profitability of a population of customers.

Sensitivity analyses — basically "what if" analyses applied across an entire range on a predictor characteristic — are a powerful planning tool. For example, if we have a model that predicts product purchase as a function of, among other things, product price, then it may be highly illuminating to predict purchase at several different price points in order to assess the sensitivity of purchase to changes in price.

Good presentation graphics are essential to any analytic system. But graphics are not just for making slick presentations. The ability to easily plot trends, to visually portray relationships in cross-tabulations, or to show sensitivity curves can be a powerful analytic tool in and of itself. Graphical display is particularly useful as a device for summarizing large amounts of aggregate data in an easily digested form.

The ability to regroup and reweigh data is an important feature supporting any of the above aggregate analyses. Filtering out customers from your analyses who are of little interest, creating new variables from the data, and weighting customers to reflect their relative importance to you are all the kinds of support functions that must be present in your M-CIS to give you real flexibility in exploring your data.

There are two kinds of tools that are useful in analyzing individual customers: profiling and searching. Profiling is the description of the customer in terms of multiple characteristics at once. The system should not only provide a consistent and readable format for displaying the information, but should also be able to highlight any characteristic on which the customer is unusual. This latter capability requires statistical techniques for comparing individuals to norms.

Searching is any technique that helps you identify customers of interest on some dimension. Sorting customers on their recent purchase volume is a simple form of searching, providing a list of the highest volume customers. A comprehensive M-CIS will be a powerful tool for your sales force to use in identifying prospects and gaining an initial understanding of their distinguishing characteristics.

Now that we have a good idea of what properties an M-CIS has in addition to the benefits it gives you, you would probably like to know what you, as a manager, can do to facilitate the creation of an M-CIS.

SOME ADVICE ON CONSTRUCTING AN M-CIS

There are a number of steps you can take to make sure that the M-CIS you create will be useful and productive, as well as cost-effective. Probably the most important determinant of the success of an information system is the presence of an effective internal champion — a "true believer" who is an advocate for the system. Such a person will not only press for support and funding for the system, but will proselytize — making sure people are aware of its utility and providing training and support. This person will also make sure the system grows in useful directions. Without such a person, the system may not reach its full potential.

Beyond finding a champion, it is extremely important that you involve potential users of the system in its design and development. You should identify units in your company that will be most likely to use the system and individuals who are expert in the activities of those units. Pull groups of such individuals together in one or more working sessions.

In these sessions, identify their activities and where information would be most helpful to them. What types of information would have the largest impact on their decisions and over what time frames? What kinds of analyses of the data would they like to see, assuming the data were available? What kinds of links between different information sources would be useful? Find out about the kinds of reports and displays that they would find most helpful. Explore the issues of access and security: Who needs access, and how often do they need it? Must the analyses be done real-time in an interactive fashion, or can they be batch processed? How frequently should the data be updated?

In these sessions, it is important to establish priorities on information needs. You probably cannot do everything at once, and you probably do not really want to even if you could. There is a cost to incorporating information in the system. Make sure the information is needed. If possible, get experts to help establish the benefits of each type of data in terms of money savings, productivity increases, or revenue generation. Then assess the costs of providing those data and carry out at least a rudimentary cost-benefit analysis.

Using your prioritizations and, if available, cost-benefit analyses, decide what is essential to incorporate and what you will definitely include but must put off. Use any information you already have in place, if it fits in with your priorities. Plan on phasing the system in slowly, but plan for future growth of the system as well.

Avoid unnecessary complexity in the system. When dealing with systems analysts, trust your own reactions as a barometer of the understandability of the system. If you do not understand it, it is likely that others will not either. People do not use what they do not understand.

Involve your users in the evaluation of the system as well. Monitor use of system components. If there are parts of the system that are not being used, find out why. If something is not working right, find out why not and change it. If it cannot be fixed, get rid of it.

User surveys are an important form of evaluation of the usefulness of the system. Look for achievement or failure on the issues explored in the early design meetings. What needs are being met? Which ones are not being met? What impact is the system having on people's productivity? On the quality of work they are doing? On their quality of life? How are they using the system? How satisfied are they with different parts of it? Which parts are unnecessary or too complicated?

Finally, when evaluating the system, consider the following questions:

- Does the system support the needs of management? Does it have support from top management and key users?
- Does it promote and encourage a market-driven perspective in your company?
- Is it manageable and cost effective?
- Does it facilitate coordination among users and improve communication among planners? Does it increase understanding and control of resources? Is it being actively used in decision making?
- Are its goals and potential benefits well communicated?

- Is it flexible? Can it be updated, modified, or adjusted as new data become available or as your objectives, challenges, and goals change?

A SUMMARY OF MARKET-DRIVEN CUSTOMER INFORMATION SYSTEMS

To make it work, you need a champion for your M-CIS. You need to keep it simple and to build gradually, using your priorities as a guide. You absolutely must involve your potential users from the start. Their input into design is invaluable, and their feedback during evaluation of the system is critical. Think of the users as though they were customers in your internal market, and think "market driven."

Ideally, your M-CIS contains a customer data record for *all* current and potential customers, with many types of customer information from multiple sources — firmographics, purchase data, channel usage, media viewing, product perceptions, product preferences, organizational decision-making structures, and customer needs. While the actual structure of your database does not necessarily follow this ideal format, it should at least provide the same capabilities. Foremost among these capabilities is the ability to examine relationships and to create links between diverse items of information.

The system must be easily updated and modified, with methods of imputation of missing data, when appropriate and feasible. It must be user friendly or it will not get used. It must provide analytics that support the analyses desired, common examples being cross-tabulation, trend analyses, prediction modeling, and the individual customer analyses of searching and profiling.

These features of an M-CIS all must provide support to the

planning, sales, market research, and monitoring functions. The M-CIS should provide information that cuts across the functional boundaries of marketing, product development, and sales.

Being market-driven requires access to customer information, particularly information on customer needs. The primary purpose of a customer information system is to provide you with access to needs data and to allow you to relate customer needs to other characteristics. These capabilities facilitate your use of needs data in marketing decisions, which is the essence of being market driven.

8

GUIDELINES FOR IMPLEMENTATION: A HOLISTIC FRAMEWORK

No matter how dynamic the segmentation analyses or inspired the strategic and tactical applications appear to be, they must be implemented effectively to achieve the benefits of the approach — timely response to market needs and requirements, continuous competitive advantage, and reduced cost in hard dollars and missed opportunities.

Among the most important lessons we have learned is that successful implementation starts at the planning stages before any data are collected. At this time, it is important to avoid an exclusive focus on near-term market research-related activities. Instead, you must step back and adopt a long-range, holistic vision of the interaction between the information platform and analytics and the organizational environment that will be essential to successful implementation.

To help you get from here to there with the most gain and

least pain, we begin this chapter with a discussion of a holistic framework for planning implementation. Along the way, we identify barriers you can expect to encounter, and we provide guidelines for overcoming these barriers. We conclude with descriptions of the nuts and bolts of implementation at several critical functional levels including product development, marketing, and sales.

The overall objective is straightforward: Identify customer needs and translate these needs into products and services that deliver differentiating value to the customer in a timely, cost-effective manner. To successfully put this objective into operation, three key elements of implementation must work together interactively: (1) a market-based information platform and delivery system, (2) the requisite tools for reducing this information to a form that supports fast, accurate decision making, and (3) a supportive organizational environment that can transform decisions into effective actions. These elements of implementation are illustrated in Exhibit 41.

MARKET-BASED INFORMATION PLATFORM AND DELIVERY SYSTEMS

The foundation for implementation is constructed upon current, reliable information designed to support market-driven decisions. Examples of these data include:

- benchmark surveys identifying among other things, customer needs and requirements, firmographic profiles, opportunity and sizing estimates, decision-making processes, and distribution and advertising preferences
- customer sales and service profiles, including installed product units, revenue, and service contacts by customer

- tracking data, updating customer needs and requirements, segment sizing and opportunity distributions, and firmographic characterizations
- product-based research such as customer preferences for features, willingness to pay, and vendor preferences
- competitive assessment data including product sales, market share, product feature, and pricing profiles

Exhibit 41
IMPLEMENTATION ELEMENTS

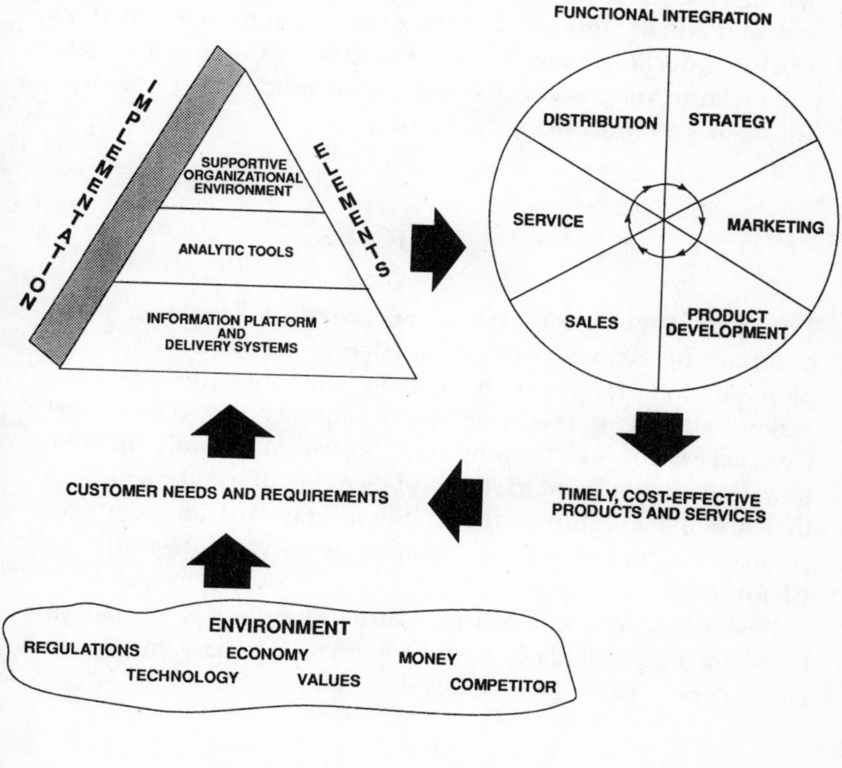

- other relevant decision support data such as delivery cost data, distribution channel profiles, and personnel skills information.

In our experience, a single source of market information can reduce time-consuming internal debates related to differences of opinion about the nature of the market and what the market wants. However, these data are of little value if they are not easily accessible to those who must use them.

As we noted in Chapter 7, one type of accessibility can be insured by installing an automated market-information system that delivers data on request to desktop workstations. A second, and equally important, type of accessibility is enabled by providing desktop analytic tools that permit the user to easily reduce large volumes of customer information into forms that can readily support decision making.

ANALYTIC TOOLS

Timely decision making based on accurate information about customer needs is a critical objective of our approach to implementation. However, to achieve this objective, decision makers at various levels within the applications chain must have access to, and training on, the use of friendly analytic tools that enable them to slice and dice the information in ways that are meaningful to them. Some standard analytic procedures for customer information systems were described in Chapter 7.

Beyond those standard procedures, there are four analytic tools that are particularly useful when you are analyzing needs-based survey data. These tools include:

1. A standard statistical package

Standardized off-the-shelf statistical packages — preferably interactive — permit users to perform conventional cross-tabular and multivariate analyses on data within the information platform. Today, all of these packages are available for PCs, minis, and mainframe use. Regardless of the computing environment, users prefer the convenience of timely desktop access, ease of use, and graphics.

2. A simple, low-cost method for classifying a customer into a segment real time

Once the benchmark segmentation has been completed, you will want the ability to assign customers to segments on the fly with an acceptable degree of accuracy. There are several reasons why you would want this capability.

First, in direct or telemarketing contacts, salespersons will want to quickly classify a customer into a segment and then customize the selling message according to the needs identified for that segment by the benchmark segmentation effort. The ability to quickly customize the message will improve the odds that a sale will be made.

For instance, suppose an electric utility service representative or telemarketing professional could ask a few questions of prospective customers and on the basis of their response determine that the customer was highly likely to be a member of the Proactives segment we described in Chapter 3. A utility service representative could tailor the message around the needs of a Proactive, mentioning how the product will help the customer provide superior service, enable line management to control costs, and improve the efficiency of operations. In the case of the telemarketing application, a script could be automatically customized to incorporate the needs that are important to Proactives.

Second, when tracking segment membership distributions

over time or monitoring the segment membership of buyers to assess your performance in target markets, you will want a quick, cost-effective means of assigning segment membership. For instance, if you are monitoring performance, you may want the buyer to answer a short set of questions that can be used to assign the customer to a segment.

We developed such a tool for the Electric Power Research Institute (EPRI) for use in assigning customers to their segments. Called CLASSIFY™, this software contains a transparent statistical procedure that calculates probabilities of EPRI segment membership based on the responses a customer provides to a limited set of needs-related questions. The questions that are included in the software represent a small discriminating set of questions derived from a larger questionnaire used in the EPRI benchmark segmentation effort. CLASSIFY™ is available in diskette form for real-time classification of customers by utility field salespersons using notebooks or laptops. It can also be used to process survey forms containing the limited list of discriminating needs questions, and it can be used in conjunction with telephone interviewing to classify customers.

3. A reasonably reliable method for prequalifying customers into segments prior to any contact

The objective of this tool is to assign all of your customers or prospects to segments without asking them any needs-based questions. As Exhibit 42 illustrates, the ability to prequalify customers on segment membership would enable sales management to divide customers or prospects within service territories into segments and prioritize contacts based on strategic opportunities identified in the benchmark segmentation effort.

The major benefit of customer prequalification is that it permits targeted selling, which in turn creates selling efficiencies. For example, suppose the benchmark segmentation effort indicates that customers in Segments 1, 6, 7, and 9 are prime candidates for your products. Assignment of specific customers to segments would enable you to identify those customers or prospects who are likely to be members of Segments 1, 6, 7, and 9. With this information in hand, you can assign those priority customers to your sales force. Armed with an understanding of the needs that are driving interest in your products, the sales force can call upon these customers. Tar-

Exhibit 42
PREQUALIFICATION OF CUSTOMERS/PROSPECTS

CUSTOMER/PROSPECT LIST

NAME	ADDRESS	SEGMENT
THE LIMITED	191 MAIN ST.	①
CHEZ COMFORT	751 NORTH ST.	4
WALLY WORLD	19 FUN HILL DRIVE	5
McDONALD'S	89 ELVIS RD.	⑥
HOLY REDEEMER	361 ELM ST.	2
WIDGET MFG.	385 OAK AVE.	8
NCNB	352 MAIN ST.	⑦
FAMILY DOLLAR	187 MARKET ST.	①
LEE'S HOAGIES	17TH ST.	6
MARIANNE SHOP	ECHELON MALL	5
ELECTRONIC BOUTIQUE	81 HOLLY OAK	⑦

○ PRIORITY SEGMENTS

SALES ASSIGNMENTS

BOB SMITH

NAME	ADDRESS	SEGMENT
THE LIMITED	191 MAIN ST.	1
McDONALD'S	89 ELVIS RD.	6
NCNB	352 MAIN ST.	7
FAMILY DOLLAR	187 MARKET ST.	1
ELECTRONIC BOUTIQUE	81 HOLLY OAK	7

BILL JONES
(Segment Specialists)

NAME	ADDRESS	SEGMENT
ED'S LANDSCAPING	18TH ST.	9
CUT ABOVE	ANN DR.	9
COOL CLIPS	MAIN ST.	9
OLTS OIL	COLLINGS AVE.	9
7-11	MILL ST.	9
WILSON'S	PINE AVE.	9

geted, focused selling efforts like this produce higher rates of sales per contact than standard shotgun approaches. Moreover, increased sales success rates tend to build a positive attitude among salespeople, which in turn reinforces their willingness to use the needs-based technique. Finally, a happy sales force experiences lower rates of turnover.

In the course of our work for EPRI, we created a tool that produces a reasonably accurate segment assignment. The tool is called LINK™. LINK™ is based on statistical relationships between accessible firmographic information and segment membership. These statistical relationships are determined from the benchmark segmentation data. For example, we determined in our work for EPRI that knowledge about a customer's industry type (SIC), employee size, monthly electric usage, amount of occupied space, and the relative speed of bill payment enabled us to correctly predict segment membership at rates over three times that of random chance alone. In other words, if a salesperson calls on a customer prequalified as a member of Segment 1, he or she can expect the assignment to be correct three times more often than without the prequalification. Once the contact has been established, the salesperson can use the CLASSIFY™ questions to improve the accuracy of segmentation assignment to over eight times that of chance alone.

4. A method for estimating the attractiveness, to segment members, of various packages of product features and functionality

Once a needs-based MBS approach has been adopted, it will be important to relate product development activities to segments, particularly target opportunity segments. In addition, product developers will need to understand how to package or repackage features and price products so that the product lines fit the needs of target segments.

For instance, an electric utility might offer its business customers a program whereby the utility would retain the option of interrupting service when the peak demand on their system reaches a brownout threshold. As Exhibit 43 illustrates, the utility has numerous options for configuring such a program. The issue product developers must confront is which of these options is likely to be most attractive to customers in designated target segments.

To address this issue, the utility could conduct primary market research using conjoint analysis. As we have described before, conjoint analysis is a technique that attempts to replicate the trade-off process customers use when making purchase decisions. These data can be incorporated into a choice model to enable product developers to run "what if" simulations and estimate purchase volumes or revenues for different

Exhibit 43
THE USE OF A CHOICE MODEL
TO SIMULATE PRODUCT PACKAGE OPTIONS

(INTERRUPTIBLE LOAD PROGRAM PACKAGE OPTIONS)

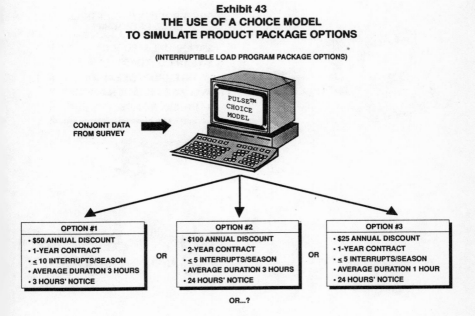

OPTION #1		OPTION #2		OPTION #3
• $50 ANNUAL DISCOUNT		• $100 ANNUAL DISCOUNT		• $25 ANNUAL DISCOUNT
• 1-YEAR CONTRACT	OR	• 2-YEAR CONTRACT	OR	• 1-YEAR CONTRACT
• ≤ 10 INTERRUPTS/SEASON		• ≤ 5 INTERRUPTS/SEASON		• ≤ 5 INTERRUPTS/SEASON
• AVERAGE DURATION 3 HOURS		• AVERAGE DURATION 3 HOURS		• AVERAGE DURATION 1 HOUR
• 3 HOURS' NOTICE		• 24 HOURS' NOTICE		• 24 HOURS' NOTICE

OR...?

201

configurations of attributes and features for products and services. The inclusion of a short set of questions like CLASSIFY™ in the survey with the conjoint exercise will create a connection between the product packaging preference of an individual and segment membership. As Exhibit 44 indicates, once this connection is established, the choice model can generate estimates of purchase or revenues by segment.

We developed a tool that combines CLASSIFY™ with a choice model for EPRI. This tool is called PULSE™. PULSE™ requires survey data input that includes a conjoint and segment membership. PULSE™ produces estimates of preference for various product feature packages by segment.

Exhibit 44
DEMAND ESTIMATES BY PACKAGE AND SEGMENT

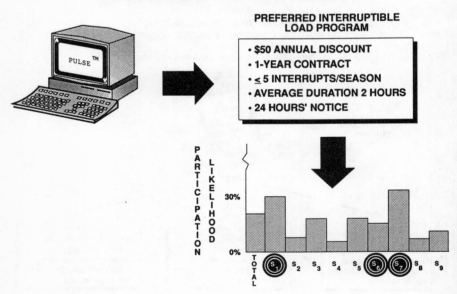

THE ORGANIZATIONAL ENVIRONMENT

Successful implementation of a needs-based approach to markets frequently requires substantive yet subtle changes in the organizational environment. The degree and amplitude of required change is predicated on the presence of barriers to the achievement of the primary objectives — the translation of customer needs into the timely, cost-effective delivery of products and services that provide differentiating value to the customer. Typically, these barriers are discovered in two areas of the organization environment — the process and the attitudes. To help you recognize and respond to these barriers, we describe some of the barriers we have observed and provide some guidelines for addressing them.

Attitudinal Barriers and Remedial Guidelines

The most serious barriers to success are attitudinal. Attitudes related to the primacy of product, turf protection, and fear of change frequently conspire to create organizational inertia. There are no quick fixes that will help you overcome these attitudinal barriers. The most effective and enduring methods for changing attitudes are education, understanding, ownership, and success. Among these, success is the most effective medicine. If it works or if people are convinced it will work, then self-interest will take over and support will occur. Nevertheless, education and ownership are prerequisites to both real or perceived success.

To obtain the cooperation that is necessary to put the applications described in Chapters 5 and 6 into operation, it is essential that management in marketing, product development, sales, and service be educated about the applications and benefits of the MBS framework. We have found that a successful education effort requires active, repeated promotion, and presentation of a story line that simplifies the approach and focuses on the benefits. Understanding and acceptance can be expedited by directly involving members of key applications functional units in the benchmark segmentation effort. Involvement not only creates acceptance but also ownership — a feeling of responsibility for the success of subsequent applications. Moreover, ownership combats fear of change and perceived threats to turf.

Cross-functional Integration as a Remedy to Structure and Process Barriers

In addition to attitudes, functional divisions of labor embedded in organizational structure and process protocols can be a significant barrier to successful implementation. To get the greatest return from the applications, it is critical that functional units such as marketing, product development, sales, service, distribution, and manufacturing work together in an integrated manner. Exhibit 45 illustrates the interdependencies of functional units, information tools, and applications.

Integration in this context starts with a shared vision that needs-based MBS is the most effective way to achieve success in the future. Beyond the shared vision, integration requires that all relevant functional units concentrate their efforts initially on common target needs-based segments. While the availability of, and access to, a common segmentation database facilitates integration, sharing of new information related to segments such as product feature preferences produces an efficient and coordinated result.

204

In most cases, functional integration will require subtle yet substantive changes in the processes and behavior associated with the way existing organizational structures interact with each other and the customer. To help you think about some of the nuts and bolts of functional integration, we conclude this chapter by describing how key functional units such as product development, marketing, and sales can use and share segmentation data, as well as the tools described above to achieve the

Exhibit 45
INTEGRATION MODEL

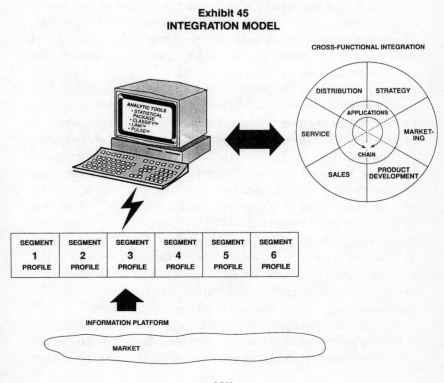

CROSS-FUNCTIONAL INTEGRATION

DISTRIBUTION STRATEGY
APPLICATIONS
SERVICE MARKET-ING
CHAIN
SALES PRODUCT DEVELOPMENT

ANALYTIC TOOLS
• STATISTICAL PACKAGE
• CLASSIFY™
• LINK™
• PULSE™

| SEGMENT 1 PROFILE | SEGMENT 2 PROFILE | SEGMENT 3 PROFILE | SEGMENT 4 PROFILE | SEGMENT 5 PROFILE | SEGMENT 6 PROFILE |

INFORMATION PLATFORM

MARKET

205

objective produce timely, cost-effective products and services that meet customer needs.

PRODUCT DEVELOPMENT AND R&D

Broadly speaking, product development and R&D activities involve the refinement of existing products, extensions to existing products, and the design and production of new products. Working within the MBS framework, product development can use the benchmark segmentation effort and subsequent tracking surveys to identify and prioritize unmet needs and requirements relative to strategic markets and segments. These prioritized needs and requirements can be translated into proposed refinements in existing products, product-line extensions, and new product concepts.

Before significant investments are made, product development must determine the relative attractiveness, revenue, and profit potential of alternative refinements, extensions, and new products in the context of the strategic segments and existing product portfolios. The analytic tools can be used to expedite action on these objectives. For instance, at various times during the year, people in product development can piggyback research questions onto segment-tracking surveys, or they can append the short-form CLASSIFY™-like questions to any customer research they conduct. The research findings can provide an evaluation of the relative attractiveness, as well as the revenue and profitability potential for each alternative by each needs segment. Exhibit 46 illustrates the process whereby product development can use the tools.

Because the analyses are systematic and the criteria for selecting among alternative product configuration choices are common across products, consistency with the target segment objectives is ensured. Product-to-market cycle times can be shortened by sharing the research with marketing. Marketing can use the information to develop positioning, promotion, pricing, and distribution plans for the emerging products.

MARKETING

Marketing has responsibility for coordinating the marketing mix across products and markets relative to the target segments. Marketing mix activity typically includes:

- product (definitions and features from product development)
- product pricing
- market and product positioning
- distribution channel selection and tactical partnerships
- sales support

Since we have described how the needs-based framework can be used to define and guide the marketing mix in Chapters 5 and 6, we will limit our discussion here to the role of marketing in implementing these applications.

Integrating Market Mix Management

As Exhibit 47 demonstrates, nowhere is the need for integration more obvious than in market mix management. First of all, marketing mix activities are highly dependent on each other for information and analytics. For instance, those who are responsible for positioning should be knowledgeable about the information and analytics that are used to determine

Exhibit 46
USE OF MBS TOOL TO SUPPORT PRODUCT DEVELOPMENT

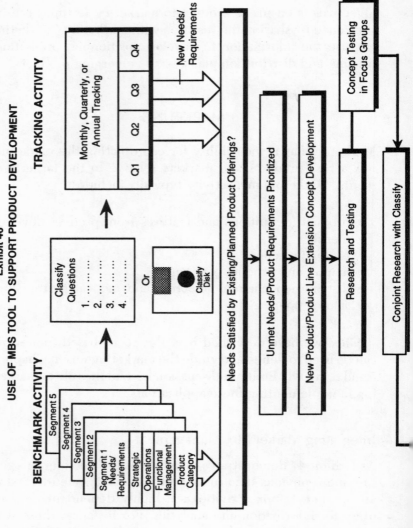

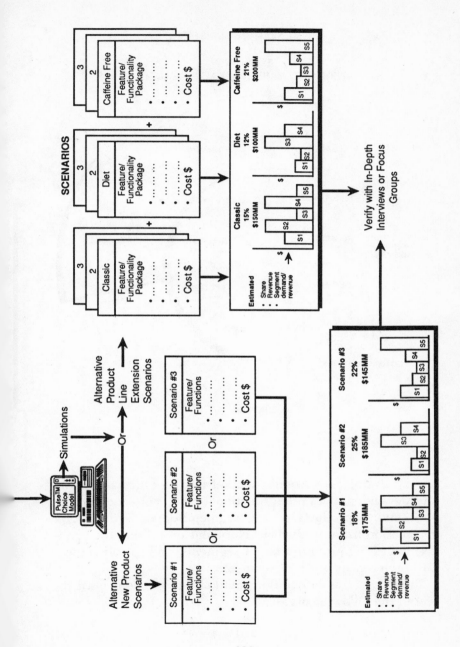

Exhibit 47
INTEGRATED MARKET MIX MANAGEMENT

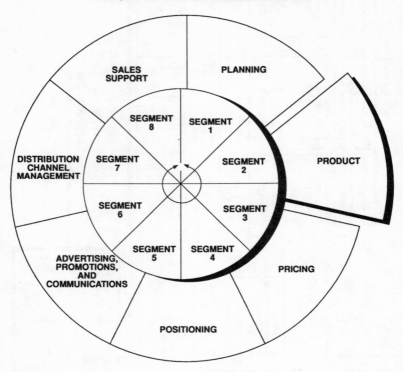

pricing strategies. Secondly, market mix activities are highly interdependent with other functional units. For example, the positioning of products to target segments depends, in part, on information from product development describing the product, indicating proposed target segments, and specifying feature preferences of target segments.

To achieve this integration, market management must invest in the following areas:

- open lines of personal communications with other functional units, as well as activity areas or groups within the mix
- the sharing of information and analytics across functional units and within mix activity areas
- automated systems that facilitate the first two points
- coordination of activities to achieve timely delivery of value to target segments

There are internal organization structures for achieving integrated market mix management. One option is to establish a single market mix management organization with cross-segment responsibility. In this model, marketing mix activities are not assigned to marketing management responsible for any one segment. Instead, the activities are integrated across segments, as Exhibit 47 shows. The strength of this approach is its strategic focus on all target segments and the interrelationships of marketing actions across the segments. For instance, a positioning strategy is designed such that its effects on all target segments are taken into account. The weakness of this cross-segment management approach is its tendency to overlook the development of specific differentiated marketing mix strategies for individual segments, thereby sacrificing some of the power of the MBS approach.

A second alternative is to organize the marketing mix around segments. Under this model, each segment would have its own dedicated, integrated marketing mix team. The advantage of this approach is that it can optimize returns within segments. The disadvantages include the additional layer of management necessary to coordinate activities across segments.

In our judgment, both models are valid; however, we think the first model is most appropriate at the beginning. Only after the first model is working effectively should microintegrated segment management be attempted.

Product Pricing

Pricing activities involve the specification of unit prices, as well as pricing structures such as fixed and variable pricing, discount plans, and bundled, as well as unbundled, pricing tactics for each product in the portfolio for each segment.

To define product unit prices effectively within and across segments, as well as the appropriate mix of portfolio pricing structures, the marketing pricing group must have information that allows them to estimate competitive price-demand curves for various pricing structures within the product and across the product portfolio for each strategic segment and all strategic segments as a group. In addition, the pricing group must be able to estimate overhead and expenses for each product and each segment in order to factor profitability into the pricing equation.

The benchmark segmentation and tracking and monitoring data, as well as the research findings from efforts to determine customer preferences for product design, can provide those responsible for pricing with a body of segment-level information that can be used to quickly, effectively, and systematically specify and modify pricing. Exhibit 48 outlines an integrated process for defining pricing strategies within and across segments and products.

Market and Product Positioning

The objective of market and product positioning activities is to develop messages that can be used in advertising, promotion, sales, and even distribution channel selection, to favorably

Exhibit 48
PRICING REVIEW PROCESS

CURRENT PRODUCTS

**BENCHMARK DATA/
PORTFOLIO VALUE ANALYSES**

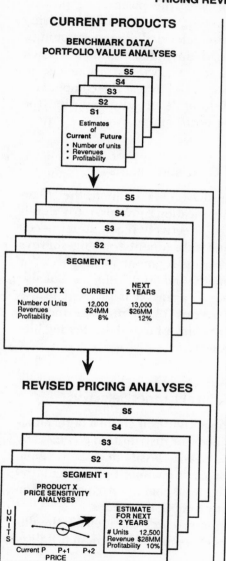

S5
S4
S3
S2
S1
Estimates
of
Current   Future
• Number of units
• Revenues
• Profitability

S5
S4
S3
S2
SEGMENT 1

PRODUCT X	CURRENT	NEXT 2 YEARS
Number of Units	12,000	13,000
Revenues	$24MM	$26MM
Profitability	8%	12%

REVISED PRICING ANALYSES

S5
S4
S3
S2
SEGMENT 1

PRODUCT X
PRICE SENSITIVITY
ANALYSES

U N I T S

Current P   P+1   P+2
PRICE

ESTIMATE FOR NEXT 2 YEARS
Units   12,500
Revenue $28MM
Profitability 10%

NEW PRODUCTS/PRODUCT LINE EXTENSIONS/VALUE ANALYSES

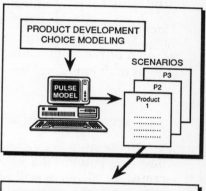

PRODUCT DEVELOPMENT
CHOICE MODELING

PULSE
MODEL

SCENARIOS
P3
P2
Product
1
....
....
....
....

PRODUCT RECOMMENDED BY PRODUCT DEVELOPMENT

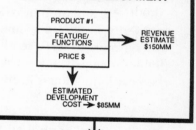

PRODUCT #1
FEATURE/
FUNCTIONS
PRICE $

→ REVENUE ESTIMATE $150MM

ESTIMATED
DEVELOPMENT
COST → $85MM

PRICING GROUP ANALYSIS

STEPS

1. Review product development estimates of revenue and cost

2. Estimate marketing costs by segment

3. Calculate profitability

4. Recalibrate price

5. Recommend final pricing plan

differentiate products in the minds of potential buyers within and across segments. Like pricing, the positioning process must integrate data from benchmark, tracking, and monitoring and product development research to define positionings. Once potential positionings are defined, focus groups for each segment can be recruited using a CLASSIFY®-like instrument. These focus groups can be used to test the competitive strength of the statements. Exhibit 49 broadly describes the process of defining and testing positionings.

Advertising, Promotion, and Communications

Once the positioning messages have been defined, the advertising, promotion, and communications groups must determine which channels will most effectively reach target needs segments. The benchmark and subsequent tracking surveys can be used, not only to identify segment preferences for advertising and promotional media and other vehicles, but also to specify usage behaviors. Once again, it is prudent to use focus groups to test the effectiveness of the message and medium. Obviously, it is most cost efficient to roll this testing into the positioning focus group efforts.

Distribution Channel and Tactical Partner Selection

Distribution channel selection activities include a determination of segment-level preferences for distribution channels by product or portfolios of products, an assessment of the revenue and profitability potential for each channel by segment and product, negotiations with potential channel partners, and an evaluation of alternative joint promotional tactics.

The benchmark segmentation research can identify the distribution channel preferences of segments by product. Subse-

Exhibit 49
PROCESS FOR SELECTING POSITIONINGS

OVERALL POSITIONING

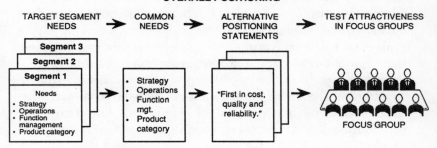

SENIOR EXECUTIVE POSITIONING

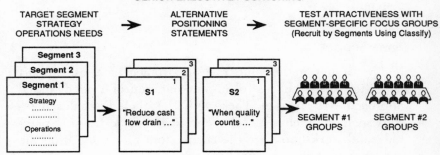

FUNCTIONAL MANAGEMENT POSITIONINGS

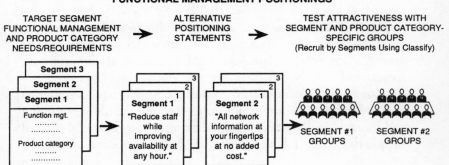

215

quent tracking and monitoring can be used to evaluate the effectiveness of distribution channel choices you have made and direct changes in channel partners. Finally, product development research can be integrated to define channel preferences for new products.

Beyond these conventional applications, you can leverage the segmentation data (e.g., segment-level channel preferences and needs) in the negotiations with candidate partners. In addition, the needs information can be used to support the development of joint promotions. However, should you use distribution channel partners, you might want to require them to administer a CLASSIFY™-like questionnaire to all buyers so that you can monitor channel effectiveness by product and segment.

Sales Support

You must not undervalue the importance of sales support activities to the successful implementation of a needs-based approach to the market. These activities, including sales materials such as brochures, telemarketing scripts, training manuals, and workshops, are the cornerstones for translating the approach into effective field action.

Like other market mix activities, sales support materials must be developed around the target needs segments and product portfolios, as well as relevant horizontal and vertical markets (e.g., national accounts or financial services). As an example, let us take a quick look at how sales training might be structured.

To get buy-in from sales veterans and encourage compliance with segmentation objectives, sales training should be ongoing and hierarchically structured, beginning with a workshop and supporting materials that describe the needs-based approach, its objectives, and benefits. Subsequent training modules might become increasingly more specialized. For example, an overview module might describe the needs and product port-folio opportunities related to each segment. Another module could train salespeople how to recognize a segment member when they see one. And, finally, specialized modules might focus on how to use needs to increase selling effectiveness in various vertical markets within each needs segment.

SALES

Whenever we talk to outstanding salespeople about what makes them successful, we hear common story lines: "I try to learn as much as I can about my customers before I talk to them for the first time." "When I talk to customers, I listen to what they say about their needs." "I try to shape selling themes around the needs of each customer — one suit doesn't fit all." "I've learned that the product features don't sell, it's how I relate the product to their business and technical needs that counts." "If I am talking to upper-level management, I try to focus on how the product will benefit the business, but when I talk to an MIS director, I talk features." "To maintain a lasting relationship with my clients, I have to constantly stay on top of their changing needs. If I don't, the competition hands me my lunch."

In many respects, the needs approach and companion tools, such as CLASSIFY™ and LINK™, mirror the best practices of star salespeople. They identify business- and product-related needs and requirements. They allow you to locate groups of customers with similar needs and propensities to purchase your products. They support tailored positionings for each customer, as well as different influencers within the customer organization. Finally, if you track segment membership and monitor needs over time, you can capture the changes that star salespeople say are so important to maintaining account control. For these reasons, needs-based segmentation is not only an excellent vehicle for supporting your best salespeople but also for institutionalizing the best practices of your stars. However, if these were the only reasons for making needs-based segmentation an integral part of your sales operations, we would counsel you to go hire a bunch of stars, if you could find them.

While you will want to integrate the needs approach into your sales activities to achieve your strategic objectives, segmentation tools can save you money and increase revenues by improving your hit rate among prospects. For example, you can use a LINK™-like tool (the statistical equation that establishes the relationship between known firmographic characteristics and segment membership) to preassign customers to segments. Preassignment allows you to construct a list of prospects prioritized according to strategic target market selections. If you use mail to reach your customers, then you can customize the mailer to appeal to the needs of the segment to which the customer is assigned. If you use direct sales techniques, when sales personnel contact preassigned prospects either by telephone or in person, they can administer or ask the customers to complete a CLASSIFY™-like questionnaire (a short list of questions that reliably defines segment membership) to validate segment membership. By the way, customers tell us they like it when a salesperson starts off by asking about their needs.

Having quickly verified the segment in which the customer is located, the salesperson can refer to the sales support materials prepared by marketing (these should be committed to memory) to profile and prioritize the strategic-, operations-, function-, and product-related needs of the customer, as well as to list the portfolio of products the customer is most likely to purchase.

In the present and subsequent contacts or proposals, the salesperson can use this information to customize positioning messages and selling platforms around the customer's needs and product requirements. Even more important, the relative importance of segment-member needs across the strategy, operations, function, and product dimensions will signal the salesperson as to whether senior management or the target functional organization will be directly or indirectly involved in the sale. In the case of a customer classified in a segment in which strategic needs are particularly strong, the salesperson is forewarned that he or she will have to position the product around strategic needs, as well as function- and product-level needs. In such a situation, it is likely that a successful sale will require a personal meeting with senior executives, in addition to a traditional functional-level buyer such as the telecommunications manager.

In cases in which telemarketing is used, CLASSIFY℠-like questions can precede a scripted pitch that can be customized to insert needs and products depending on the segment to which the customer is assigned and the level (e.g., senior executive, functional manager) of the person to whom the telemarketer is talking.

As an aside, whenever CLASSIFY℠-type questions are administered, you should store the results in a centralized database such as a customer information system. Such a corporate file can serve many uses. For instance, if a customer calls to inquire about a product or service, the customer's file can be brought up on a screen along with other pertinent information, such as billing, to more effectively answer the customer's question or convert the inquiry into a selling opportunity. More important, in an era of high turnover in sales, capturing and automating access to information that often resides in the head of a departed salesperson is a recovered asset — a form of insurance for preserving client service continuity.

Now that we have given you a taste of some needs-based segment sales applications, let's take a look at how you should organize your selling activities in an environment that is market needs oriented.

The Sales Organization Infrastructure

It doesn't matter whether you organize sales by geography, product, industry, size, or all of the above, you probably do not have to change your sales organization to use the needs-based approach. What must change are the bases for measuring and compensating the sales force. To accomplish strategic segmentation objectives, you must establish sales volume objectives (e.g., unit/$) for a designated product mix or portfolio within each target segment. Incentives are then paid out on the basis of sales performance within target segments.

For those of you with a large diversified customer base who want to reorganize sales, you can structure field sales around segments. In each sales territory, sales personnel would specialize in one or more segments. All prospects and existing customers would be preassigned according to segment membership and salesperson specialization. Quotas are then assigned and incentives paid on sales volumes within an assigned segment. At aggregate levels, branch, regional, and national sales managers also are assigned target quotas by product and compensated in large part on how well sales personnel in their territories perform against the quotas.

Sales Performance Monitoring

Regardless of whether you simply modify your existing bases for establishing quotas and paying incentives or you restructure by creating a segment-focused approach to sales, performance measurement will require you to monitor sales volumes within each segment monthly, quarterly, or annually.

Monitoring sales by segment can be accomplished in several ways. First, you can use preassigned segment designations generated by a LINK™-like tool to measure performance. For example, salesperson Jones agrees at the beginning of the year on the objectives in Exhibit 50 for target segments.

Jones is provided with a list of current and potential customers within her territory who are preassigned by a LINK™-like tool to the target segments. Performance measurement is simple. Jones must achieve sales quotas by product and segment from those firms on the list. However, because the LINK™ segment assignment is likely to be only marginally reliable (30 to 60 percent accurate), we would recommend that you use a second more reliable method for monitoring sales performance by segment.

The second method is the same as the first, except that during the selling process, field sales personnel administer a CLASSIFY™-like questionnaire to prospective customers. When the customer completes CLASSIFY™, segment assignment will be highly accurate. Obviously, to prevent cheating on the part of sales personnel, you will have to validate a sample of completed CLASSIFY™ forms for each salesperson. However, there is enormous value in imposing the use of a CLASSIFY™-like tool to monitor performance. On the one hand, CLASSIFY™ will enable you to more reliably measure corporate performance against strategic objectives. On the

Exhibit 50
ANNUAL SALES OBJECTIVES BY SEGMENT

SALES TARGETS: MS. JONES

SEGMENT 1	
Products	**Number of Units**
A	1,200
C	1,400
E	2,000

SEGMENT 2	
Products	**Number of Units**
B	4,200
C	1,850
E	3,500
F	25

LINK™-DERIVED PROSPECT LISTS

SEGMENT 1

Current Customers
* AKA Electric
  35 Main Street Baltimore, MD
  301-429-7100
  Number of units installed:
  A-22
  C-14
  E 0
  Contact:
  "Bill Bagley"
  MIS Director

SEGMENT 2

Current Customers
* Alcon Electric
  12 Elm Street
  Baltimore, MD
  301-429-2201
  Number of units installed:
  B - 45
  C - 28
  E - 57
  F - 1

SEGMENT 1

Prospects
* Albo Appliances
  721 Eagle Plaza
  Baltimore, MD
  301-765-2100

* Anco Appliances
  1800 Oyster Drive
  Baltimore, MD
  301-829-1401

SEGMENT 2

Prospects
* Al's Appliances
  1472 Maple Street
  Baltimore, MD
  301-428-1701

* GE Outlet
  78 Oak Street
  Baltimore, MD
  301-749-1800

other hand, the administration of CLASSIFY™ will create customer profiles of needs that can be preserved in a customer information system for use by sales and marketing.

Beyond Infrastructure

While the organizational infrastructure and lines of authority are important to the successful implementation, we feel compelled to remind you that organization and authority are a hollow promise without integration, education, ownership, and a shared feeling that the approach will work.

9

THE MARKET-DRIVEN COMPANY
OF THE FUTURE

We have argued in earlier chapters that emerging changes in the structure of business markets pose a serious challenge to those who sell products and services to other businesses. While some industries such as the electronics, automotive, and computer industries are already feeling the effects of these changes, no industry is likely to escape.

The talisman of these structural changes is the customer. In the evolving market, customers will become more knowledgeable about what they need from suppliers, and they will become more demanding. They will want error-free products and services that fit their needs but are simple to use and maintain. Moreover, they will want these products and services when they need them at the lowest possible price. The buzzword that customers will use to summarize these requirements will be *value*.

Increasing competition, often on a global scale, will reinforce customer leverage by generating an increase in product, feature, and service choices. Suppliers will experience higher product development costs related to shorter product life cycles. Marketing, sales, and service costs are likely to increase as well because suppliers will be forced to invest more heavily in these activities as they search for ways to differentiate themselves from the competition. Under these conditions, profit margins will be under considerable downward pressure.

To succeed in this environment, aim and execution are important. First, you must identify the markets in which customer needs are compatible with your capabilities. Then, your marketing must enlighten customers about why your products and services are right for them. Finally, you must deliver the right product mix to the right markets at the right time with acceptable margins.

In this environment, it is necessary, as much as possible, to eliminate errors, but this requires a sharply focused, disciplined process for monitoring and responding to the changing needs of the market. The discipline involves timely translation of customer needs to products and services. Furthermore, it demands effective conversion of needs to differentiated, targeted selling themes executed by market planners and management as well as field sales. Finally, the discipline requires a supportive, responsive yet integrated organizational structure and complementary processes.

To help you realize these objectives, we have provided a framework and set of procedures for describing, segmenting, and monitoring business markets. In practice, we have found that this framework reflects the complex infrastructure of business customer needs and product- and service-level requirements necessary to support product development, in a form that is intuitively sensible and usable. Because we have applied this framework successfully in different types of business product and service markets, we are confident it will work.

Throughout the previous chapters, we have described strategic and tactical applications for needs-based segmentation, outlined implementation requirements, and defined a market-information system platform designed to promote rapid cross-functional access to market-based information.

To foster a deeper understanding of how the MBS approach can benefit your business in the face of future challenges, we provide a working example of how the framework, applications, and procedures described in earlier chapters will work in concert to produce a fully market-driven company of the future. So that our example has a flavor of reality with which you can identify, we begin with a brief overview of the competitive business situation our hypothetical business faces. Following this definition of context, we describe a needs-based approach to the market. We conclude with a discussion of the specific benefits the business is likely to realize.

THE CONTEXT

The year is 1993. Our hypothetical business (PBX Inc.) is actually one line of businesses among several operating within a larger corporate infrastructure. The product line under consideration is telecommunications switching systems. Specific products within the line include three basic models of Private Branch Exchanges or PBXs. The System 30 is designed for business establishments with more than 1000 employees, the System 20 for establishments with 500 to 999 employees, and the System 10 for establishments with 50 to 499 employees. The market for these products is global.

In 1985, PBX Inc. was riding the crest of a significant overall increase in market demand for premises-based telephone switching equipment. Revenues from the three PBX products were about $500 million, while profit margins ranged from 36 percent on the high-end model to 18 percent on the low-end model. The compound annual growth rate (CAGR) during the previous five years was 30 percent. Finally, the primary competition consisted of one domestic and one Canadian PBX manufacturer, in addition to a public-switched product (Centrex) offered by local telephone companies. By 1985, PBX Inc. was capturing 46 percent of annual private- and public-switched expenditures. And while all three models were share leaders, the System 30 was capturing nearly 55 percent of all switched expenditures by large customers.

Between 1985 and 1990, market conditions began to change. Several Japanese and European manufacturers entered the PBX market. In addition, the local telephone companies made some fundamental technical changes in the Centrex product, added several key features, and extended the product line to appeal to establishments with 50 to 499 employees. As a consequence of these changes in the competitive environment, PBX Inc. began to notice a flattening of revenue, share, and margin growth in 1986 and 1987.

In 1988, when second-quarter returns projected an actual decline in revenues, share, and margins, senior management ordered product development to speed the introduction of new feature enhancements to each product. The introduction of these features in mid-1989 initiated the "Great Features War."

In response to PBX Inc.'s feature introductions, each competitor quickly began to match and increase the number of feature options available to customers. Of course, PBX Inc. felt compelled to respond in kind. Faced with a confusing array of competitive choices and feature options confounded by complex price menus, purchase cycle times increased and market growth began to subside.

During this period, 1989 to 1992, PBX Inc. experienced an increasing decline in revenues, share, and margins. In 1991, after a turnover in senior management, a new management group implemented a five-pronged strategy to reverse the trend. First, management and administrative overhead was cut in order to improve margins. Second, distribution channel partnerships were established to increase the number of sales channels. Third, the sales force was increased in the hope that more salespeople would yield more revenues. Fourth, two new services were offered as a means of generating high-margin revenues. Finally, even more features were added to the product line.

By the end of the second quarter in 1993, it was apparent to senior management that the strategy had succeeded only in slowing the decline, not in reversing the direction. At this time, a desperate management group initiated research to identify customer needs. A small group of senior managers representing marketing, sales, and product development was appointed to head up the research effort.

THE BENCHMARK RESEARCH AND ANALYTICS

During the third and fourth quarters of 1993, a benchmark study was conducted in the United States following the approach described in Chapter 3. Exhibit 51 illustrates the framework that was used as well as a sample question for each dimension.

Postsurvey analyses revealed that the telephone-switching systems market was being driven by 30 primary needs. These needs are briefly defined in Exhibit 52.

Analysis revealed that the market was composed of five customer segments, each possessing a unique configuration of needs. These segments are described briefly in Exhibit 53.

Using current product inventory data from the survey, as well as respondent estimates of purchase for the next two years, current and near future revenue and share estimates were generated to size current and potential opportunities for the market as a whole and segments in particular. Exhibits 54 and 55 describe these findings.

After the segments were defined and sized, the product requirements information was analyzed. As Exhibit 56 indicates, three separate product preference groups emerged. These product groups were then examined relative to segment membership to determine product preferences for each segment. Exhibit 57 also shows the segment-level demand for each of the product groups.

Exhibit 51
SEGMENTATION FRAMEWORK AND SAMPLE NEEDS/REQUIREMENTS

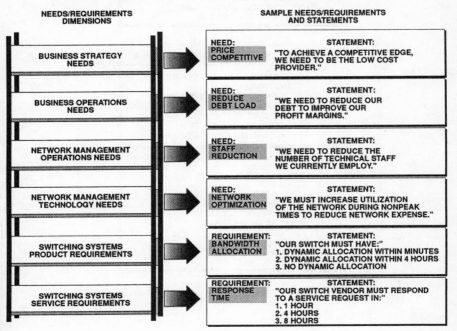

Exhibit 52
PRIMARY NEEDS

BUSINESS STRATEGY NEEDS

- QUALITY FIRST
- PRICE COMPETITIVE
- RISK ACCEPTANCE
- MARKET EXPANSION
- INNOVATION
- FAST TO MARKET
- ACCESS TO MARKET INFORMATION

BUSINESS OPERATIONS NEEDS

- GROW SKILL BASE
- REDUCE OPERATING COST
- REDUCE DEBT LOAD
- IMPROVE PERFORMANCE QUALITY
- CROSS-FUNCTIONAL INTEGRATION
- HIERARCHICAL CONTROL
- IMPROVED COMMUNICATIONS
- COST CONTROL SYSTEMS

NETWORK OPERATIONS NEEDS

- CENTRALIZE PURCHASE CONTROL
- STANDARDIZATION
- BUDGETARY CONTROL SYSTEMS
- COST REDUCTION
- STAFF REDUCTION
- INTEGRATION OF VOICE/DATA
- DESIGN AND MAINTAIN OURSELVES

NETWORK TECHNOLOGY NEEDS

- RELIABILITY
- UPTIME
- NETWORK OPTIMIZATION
- TRAFFIC MANAGEMENT
- SECURITY
- SIMPLICITY
- COMPATIBILITY
- FAULT CORRECTION

Exhibit 53
NEEDS-BASED SEGMENTS

MARKET DRIVERS

NEEDS

STRATEGIC
- QUALITY FIRST
- MARKET EXPANSION
- FAST TO MARKET
- ACCESS TO INFORMATION

BUSINESS OPERATIONS
- IMPROVE PERFORMANCE
- CROSS-FUNCTIONAL INTEGRATION
- IMPROVE COMMUNICATIONS

NETWORK OPERATIONS
- STANDARDIZE
- VOICE/DATA INTEGRATION

NETWORK TECHNOLOGY
- RELIABILITY
- UPTIME
- NETWORK OPTIMIZATION
- FAULT CORRECTION

MARGIN SENSITIVES

NEEDS

STRATEGIC
- PRICE COMPETITIVE
- RISK ACCEPTANCE

BUSINESS OPERATIONS
- REDUCE OPERATING COST
- REDUCE DEBT LOAD
- COST CONTROL SYSTEMS

NETWORK OPERATIONS
- CENTRALIZE PURCHASE CONTROL
- BUDGETARY CONTROL SYSTEMS
- COST REDUCTION

NETWORK TECHNOLOGY
- NETWORK OPTIMIZATION
- TRAFFIC MANAGEMENT
- SIMPLICITY

CENTRALIZED CONTROL FOCUSED

NEEDS

STRATEGIC
- QUALITY FIRST
- PRICE COMPETITIVE
- NO INNOVATION

BUSINESS OPERATIONS
- NO DEBT REDUCTION
- NO CROSS-FUNCTIONAL INTEGRATION
- HIERARCHICAL CONTROL

NETWORK OPERATIONS
- CENTRALIZED PURCHASE CONTROL
- STANDARDIZE
- SINGLE-VENDOR DESIGN AND MAINTENANCE

NETWORK TECHNOLOGY
- NO NETWORK OPTIMIZATION
- NO NETWORK MANAGEMENT
- COMPATIBILITY

VENDOR INDEPENDENTS

NEEDS

STRATEGIC
- PRICE COMPETITIVE
- ACCESS TO INFORMATION

BUSINESS OPERATIONS
- GROW SKILL BASE
- REDUCE OPERATING COSTS
- REDUCE DEBT
- IMPROVE COMMUNICATIONS

NETWORK OPERATIONS
- DESIGN AND MAINTAIN OURSELVES
- NO STANDARDIZATION

NETWORK TECHNOLOGY
- RELIABILITY
- UPTIME
- NETWORK OPTIMIZATION
- SIMPLICITY
- TRAFFIC MANAGEMENT

STABLE DEPENDENTS

NEEDS

STRATEGIC
- RISK AVERSE
- NO INNOVATION
- NO MARKET EXPANSION

BUSINESS OPERATIONS
- COST CONTROL SYSTEMS
- NO CROSS-FUNCTIONAL INTEGRATION
- DECENTRALIZED

NETWORK OPERATIONS
- BUDGETARY CONTROL SYSTEMS
- VOICE/DATA INTEGRATION

NETWORK TECHNOLOGY
- UPTIME
- SIMPLICITY
- COMPATIBILITY

Exhibit 54
MARKET OPPORTUNITIES AND CHANGE 1993–1995

PBX SYSTEM 30 CLASS (1000 OR MORE LINES) — 1993 / 1995 PERCENTAGE CHANGE FROM 1993

VENDORS	TOTAL REVENUE (MILLIONS)	REVENUE SHARE	SEGMENT SHARES (%)					VENDORS	PERCENT REVENUE GAIN/LOSS	SHARE POINT GAIN/LOSS	PROJECTED REVENUE GAIN/LOSS (%) BY SEGMENT				
			1	2	3	4	5				1	2	3	4	5
PBX INC.	$110	17%	9	(25)	10	(33)	15	PBX INC.	(10%)	(3)	(6)	(14)	-	(17)	-
VENDOR A	$163	25%	(44)	13	25	11	19	VENDOR A	21%	2	13	22	(33)	(20)	20
VENDOR B	$150	23%	17	(28)	(41)	6	12	VENDOR B	18%	1	(7)	45	15	-	10
VENDOR C	$98	15%	20	13	13	20	6	VENDOR C	(9%)	(3)	(14)	(5)	20	(22)	(60)
CENTREX	$98	15%	6	17	8	24	(37)	CENTREX	24%	2	(20)	(60)	(17)	14	20
OTHERS	$33	5%	4	4	3	6	11	OTHERS	28%	1	-	(60)	-	-	(67)
TOTAL	$652	100%	(28)	22	24	14	12	TOTAL	11%	/	3	(24)	16	(4)	16

PBX SYSTEM 20 CLASS (500-999 LINES) — 1993 / 1995

VENDORS	TOTAL REVENUE (MILLIONS)	REVENUE SHARE	SEGMENT SHARES (%)					VENDORS	PERCENT REVENUE GAIN/LOSS	SHARE POINT GAIN/LOSS	PROJECTED REVENUE GAIN/LOSS (%) BY SEGMENT				
			1	2	3	4	5				1	2	3	4	5
PBX INC.	$35	11%	9	18	5	13	4	PBX INC.	26	-	-	29	25	17	(200)
VENDOR A	$104	32%	(47)	13	(49)	(34)	4	VENDOR A	45	4	52	(100)	14	50	(500)
VENDOR B	$91	28%	11	(38)	25	26	(43)	VENDOR B	10	(4)	20	7	10	-	33
VENDOR C	$29	9%	9	10	7	7	18	VENDOR C	-	(2)	-	-	-	-	-
CENTREX	$59	18%	22	18	13	18	28	CENTREX	41	2	20	71	-	94	(37)
OTHERS	$7	2%	2	3	1	2	3	OTHERS	43	-	(100)	-	-	50	100
TOTAL	$325	100%	14	24	26	(27)	9	TOTAL	28	/	33	33	11	(37)	32

PBX SYSTEM 10 CLASS (50-499 LINES) — 1993 / 1995

VENDORS	TOTAL REVENUE (MILLIONS)	REVENUE SHARE	SEGMENT SHARES (%)					VENDORS	PERCENT REVENUE GAIN/LOSS	SHARE POINT GAIN/LOSS	PROJECTED REVENUE GAIN/LOSS (%) BY SEGMENT				
			1	2	3	4	5				1	2	3	4	5
PBX INC.	$26	8%	5	10	8	5	9	PBX INC.	27%	(1)	-	25	20	-	44
VENDOR A	$20	6%	16	2	4	5	7	VENDOR A	30%	2	(114)	100	(150)	50	28
VENDOR B	$18	6%	5	1	18	10	1	VENDOR B	44%	-	-	100	60	-	(100)
VENDOR C	$111	34%	16	(63)	18	20	34	VENDOR C	44%	1	(114)	27	20	150	37
CENTREX	$91	28%	13	13	(44)	12	(44)	CENTREX	51%	2	17	(130)	28	(200)	33
OTHERS	$59	18%	(45)	11	8	(48)	5	OTHERS	7%	(4)	-	22	-	-	40
TOTAL	$325	100%	14	24	18	13	(31)	TOTAL	40%	/	39	42	33	(56)	36

VENDOR A = JAPANESE VENDOR
VENDOR B = CANADIAN VENDOR
VENDOR C = EUROPEAN VENDOR
◯ = % LEADER

Exhibit 55
TOTAL MARKET OPPORTUNITY AND CHANGE 1993–1995

	TOTAL 1993 MARKET								PERCENTAGE CHANGE FROM 1993							
			SEGMENT SHARES (%)						PERCENT REVENUE GAIN/LOSS	SHARE POINT GAIN/LOSS	PROJECTED REVENUE GAIN/LOSS (%) BY SEGMENT				
VENDORS	TOTAL REVENUE (Millions)	REVENUE SHARE	1	2	3	4	5	VENDORS			1	2	3	4	5
PBX INC.	$171	13%	9	19	8	(20)	10	PBX INC.	3	(2)	(4)	2	8	(7)	(27)
VENDOR A	$287	22%	(40)	10	28	19	11	VENDOR A	48	2	29	43	(26)	(69)	43
VENDOR B	$259	20%	14	24	(32)	15	11	VENDOR B	28	-	(3)	30	19	-	26
VENDOR C	$238	18%	17	(26)	12	15	22	VENDOR C	17	(1)	6	17	17	25	22
CENTREX	$248	19%	10	16	16	19	(39)	CENTREX	38	2	19	(78)	10	67	22
OTHERS	$99	8%	10	5	4	12	7	OTHERS	16	(1)	4	31	-	4	(60)
TOTAL	$1,302	100%	21	23	23	17	16	TOTAL	23	/	14	(30)	18	29	28

○ HIGH VALUE
( ) NEGATIVE/LOSS

Once the segments and the product groups were defined, each segment was profiled to further characterize the segments. An example of these profiles is described in Exhibit 57. Similar profiles were also created for each product group.

Then the needs that defined membership in each of the segments were analyzed to determine which needs-based questions would be the most accurate predictors of segment membership. This analysis revealed that 28 questions could be used to predict segment membership correctly 95 percent of the time. These 28 questions formed the basis of CLAS-SIFY™, a short-form questionnaire for use by sales personnel to identify customer needs and verify segment membership. Even more important, CLASSIFY™ would be used to track changes in the market and monitor performance among the segments.

A similar analysis was conducted on the product requirements data. It was discovered that 11 questions could be used to define a product group preference correctly 98 percent of the time. Subsequently, these 11 questions would be appended to the CLASSIFY™ questionnaire and administered by sales personnel to help potential customers design the PBX

Exhibit 56
PRODUCT REQUIREMENTS PACKAGES

BASIC PACKAGE

- STANDARD FEATURE GROUP
- SMDR WITH ACCOUNT CODES
- CUSTOMIZED CONSOLIDATED BILLING
- MOVES AND CHANGES WITHIN 24 HOURS
- SERVICE RESPONSE WITHIN 24 HOURS
- INCOMING NUMBER IDENTIFICATION
- ONE-LEVEL PASSWORD
- NO TRAFFIC MANAGEMENT
- NO NETWORK OPTIMIZATION
- NO DYNAMIC BANDWITH ALLOCATION
- NO FAULT LOCATION
- NO VOICE/DATA INTEGRATION
- NO ERROR CHECKING

SHARE OF CUSTOMERS BY SEGMENTS

STANDARD PACKAGE

- STANDARD FEATURE GROUP
- VOICE/DATA INTEGRATION
- ERROR CHECKING
- SERVICE RESPONSE WITHIN 4 HOURS
- MOVES AND CHANGES IN 8 HOURS
- CUSTOMIZED TRAFFIC REPORTS
- FAULT LOCATION
- CUSTOMIZED CONSOLIDATED BILLING
- STANDARD SMDR
- DYNAMIC BANDWITH ALLOCATION WITHIN 8 HOURS
- ONE-LEVEL PASSWORD

SHARE OF CUSTOMERS BY SEGMENTS

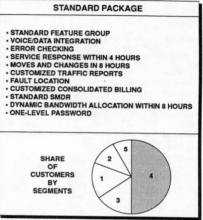

ENHANCED PACKAGE

- STANDARD FEATURE GROUP
- SERVICE RESPONSE WITHIN 4 HOURS
- DYNAMIC BANDWIDTH ALLOCATION WITHIN 4 HOURS
- CUSTOMIZED TRAFFIC REPORTS
- FAULT LOCATION
- NETWORK OPTIMIZATION
- REAL-TIME MOVES AND CHANGES
- VOICE/DATA INTEGRATION
- ERROR CHECKING
- INCOMING NUMBER IDENTIFICATION WITH DEMOGRAPHICS
- CUSTOMIZED CONSOLIDATED BILLING
- SMDR WITH ACCOUNT CODES
- TWO LEVELS OF PASSWORDS

SHARE OF CUSTOMERS BY SEGMENTS

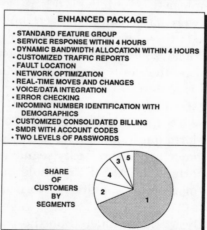

POTENTIAL TARGET SEGMENTS

234

Exhibit 57
SEGMENT PROFILES

FIRMOGRAPHIC CHARACTERISTICS	VALUE-FOCUSED EXPANSIONISTS 1	MARGIN SENSITIVES 2	CONSERVATIVE CENTRALISTS 3	SEGMENT 4	SEGMENT 5
INDUSTRY					
• MANUFACTURING/PROCESS	(20%)	10%	(30%)	5%	5%
• WHOLESALE/RETAIL	10%	(40%)	5%	5%	5%
• FINANCIAL SERVICES	(30%)	5%	5%	5%	10%
• HOTEL/RECREATION	10%	5%	(20%)	5%	(30%)
• TRANSPORT/UTILITIES	5%	5%	10%	(30%)	5%
• BUSINESS SERVICES	15%	10%	10%	(25%)	5%
• GOVERNMENT	5%	10%	15%	5%	(30%)
• EDUCATION	5%	15%	10%	20%	10%
FINANCIALS					
• DEBT LOAD	LOW	(HIGH)	LOW	(HIGH)	MED.
• CAPITAL ACCESS	HIGH	LOW	MED.	LOW	MED.
• AVERAGE MARGINS	HIGH	LOW	LOW	LOW	MED.
• REVENUE GROWTH	HIGH	LOW	(HIGH)	LOW	MED.
• MARGIN GROWTH	HIGH	LOW	LOW	LOW	LOW
• VOLATILITY	LOW	(HIGH)	(HIGH)	MED.	LOW
SIZE					
• AVERAGE # LOCATIONS	20	5	10	9	4
• AVERAGE # EMPLOYEES/ LOCATION	(75)	25	30	(50)	35
SCOPE					
• LOCAL	10	(40)	(40)	(40)	10
• REGIONAL	20	(30)	(40)	(30)	(30)
• NATIONAL	(40)	20	15	15	(40)
• GLOBAL	(30)	10	5	15	20
TECHNICAL STAFF					
• MEDIAN TECH STAFF (#)	(5)	1	2	3	3
• MEDIAN CLERICAL (#)	(6)	2	2	8	5
PRODUCT CATEGORY INVENTORY					
• AVERAGE # 30 CLASS PER ORGANIZATION	(2)	1	.8	.2	.1
• AVERAGE # 20 CLASS PER ORGANIZATION	.3	.9	(1)	(1)	.2
• AVERAGE # 10 CLASS PER ORGANIZATION	.3	.9	.6	.4	(1.5)
DECISION MAKING					
• CENTRAL/HIERARCHICAL	(HIGH)	HIGH	HIGH	LOW	LOW
• DECENTRAL/NONHIERARCHICAL	LOW	LOW	LOW	(HIGH)	(HIGH)

product they required. As you will see, these 11 product-related questions were also used to track customer requirements over time.

The final U.S. benchmark step required a discriminatory analysis to identify which firmographic characteristics could be used to most accurately predict segment membership. This analysis, called LINK℠, was to become a valuable prospecting tool for identifying likely target segment members in advance of a sales contact.

Building on the research findings in the United States, similar but more cost-efficient research was conducted in Europe and Japan. Qualitative research indicated that with only minor modifications, the needs and product requirements that defined segments and product package preferences in the United States were equally discriminating in Europe and Japan. Nonetheless, the line management team was mildly surprised to discover that the findings in Europe and Japan were consistent with those in the United States. The implication for PBX Inc. was significant. They could develop a uniform global strategy and realize significant economies in product development, marketing, and sales.

Once the global benchmark analyses were completed, the research management group met with the strategic-planning organization routinely over a three-week period to review the research findings, formulate strategic plans, develop an action plan, and specify criteria to be used for measuring and monitoring performance against plan. A brief description of the process and findings of this effort highlights the value of the benchmark needs and requirements framework as a strategic weapon.

BUILDING A BUSINESS STRATEGY

As a prerequisite to the development of a strategy, the working group reviewed market structure, opportunity, and product portfolio value analyses. These analyses were complemented by competitive assessments for each geography and segment. Finally, the group conducted an evaluation of PBX Inc.'s capabilities and compared these against market needs, product requirements, and competitive intelligence from the benchmark research and secondary sources. Included in this capabilities assessment were, among other things, the current product line, planned enhancements in the pipeline, as well as manufacturing, marketing, sales, service, and distribution channel resources.

After boiling the data, the group agreed on eight key findings that would eventually form the foundation of its strategy development.

1. Even though the premium, high-margin System 30 market would continue to grow, the fastest growth would occur within the more price-sensitive, low-margin System 10 and 20 markets.
2. In general, the Margin Sensitives, Vendor Independents, and Stable Dependents would show fastest growth in purchases over the next two years.
3. Projected growth, however, for the PBX Inc. models across these growth segments was flat or declining.
4. The major competitive threat in the growth segments would come from nonpremises-based switch products offered by the local telephone companies and new lower-priced products from the Japanese and Canadians.

5. Critical strategic, operations, and network management needs that would drive customer purchase behaviors in the future included:

- growing revenues and cash by bringing new products to the market faster and expanding markets
- creating a competitive advantage by improving communications systems and obtaining fast, accurate information about market changes
- remaining price competitive without sacrificing product quality
- improving margins and cash flow by controlling and reducing operating expenses and debt
- tightly controlling network operations budgets by reducing vendor dependence and building a small, but technically competent, network management staff to support desktop automation
- investing in technology that is simple to use, maintain, and manage; transparent to the end user; easily repaired; and adaptable to changing needs

6. Product requirements that future buyers of switched products in growth segments will seek to satisfy in order of importance include:

- customized consolidated billing
- SMDR with account codes
- moves and changes within four hours
- service response time to problems within four hours
- one-level password for security
- incoming number ID with access to demographics
- customized traffic reports
- preemptive fault location and correction

- dynamic bandwidth allocation within eight hours
- voice and data integration and error checking

7. Significant gaps exist between both current and planned PBX Inc. products and customer requirements; these gaps include:

   - customized consolidated billing
   - account codes within SMDR
   - service response time within four hours
   - incoming number ID with demographics
   - customized traffic reports
   - preemptive fault location
   - dynamic bandwidth allocation

8. While everyone at PBX Inc. knew margins were slipping, projected share and revenue declines required immediate and substantial changes in operating cost structure, target markets, product development, pricing, marketing, sales, service, and distribution.

The working group now turned to internal financial analyses. These analyses revealed that current net margins of 6 percent would decline to about 3 percent in the next two years if PBX Inc. did nothing. The group agreed that strategic and tactical decisions should be framed within a set of financial objectives:

- improve net margins to 9 percent by 1997 and 11 percent by 1999
- reduce operating expenses by 30 percent by 1997 and 50 percent by 1999

- increase revenues by 50 percent by 1997 and 100 percent by 1999
- take a one-time write-down of $30 million to pay for staff reductions
- raise cash to support investment requirements through a bond offering
- invest in the following:
  - just-in-time sales order entry, manufacturing, inventory control, and billing systems
  - an automated customer information system
  - new product development
  - sales and service consolidation and training
  - advertising and promotion

Using these financial objectives in the context of the benchmark research findings, the working group developed a strategic action plan.

STRATEGIC ACTION PLAN

The strategic action plan addressed five areas: market selection, the product portfolio and product development activities, pricing, positioning, and internal organizational requirements.

Market Selection

At the outset, everyone agreed that PBX Inc. should not attempt to satisfy the needs and requirements of all five segments. The evidence supporting this position was overwhelming: The current strategy, which was based on a shotgun approach to all markets, was obviously failing. Moreover, it was clear from the product portfolio value analysis that efforts to build products that satisfied all segments would not produce a rate of return necessary to justify the investment. Finally, and most compelling, the benchmark data indicated that future market growth was concentrated heavily in three of the five segments regardless of whether one looked at markets in a global or country-by-country context.

Based on market growth projections, competitive positioning, internal resource capabilities, and financial objectives, the group decided that PBX Inc. should focus its resources on Margin Sensitives, Vendor Independents, and Stable Dependents.

The Product Portfolio and New Product Development

The critical strategic issue of what product or mix of products to offer the target segments was the subject of extensive debate. The "old guard" argued that PBX Inc. should continue to support the existing System 30, 20, and 10 products. They pointed out that PBX Inc. could not abandon an installed base of more than 6000 units. To do so would terminally alienate current customers and undermine PBX Inc.'s credibility as a vendor customers could count on to support its products in the future. The old guard claimed that the existing product line was losing share primarily due to the failure of marketing and sales to properly position the products relative to customer needs. However, they admitted that the existing product line needed to be upgraded to make it more competitive. They estimated the cost of developing and delivering these upgrades was $30 million to $40 million.

Using the product portfolio value analyses, the projected market share data for the System 30, 20, and 10, and the results of product-requirement analyses for each target segment, a majority of the group argued successfully for a new product-line strategy.

241

While agreeing that PBX Inc. should continue to support products that were already installed, the majority proposed that existing products be phased out over an eight-year period. The old product line would be replaced by a menu of features defined by the product requirement needs of each target segment. Instead of choosing from three fixed products, each future customer could select features from a computerized menu that fit its unique needs and requirements. This menu would be upgraded based upon the results of research periodically tracking the product requirements of the market in general and the segments in particular.

Once the customer selected the features, the salesperson would download the order to manufacturing. To improve delivery time and reduce inventory costs, PBX Inc. would develop just-in-time manufacturing, delivery, and service processes. After these processes were in place (an estimated 18 months), the customer could expect delivery within 30 days, a 100 percent improvement over the fastest competitive delivery and service schedule.

Importantly, the majority claimed that this strategy could be implemented within the constraints of the financial objectives. First, 80 percent of the future market could be captured by providing a feature menu that covered Packages 1 and 2 in Exhibit 56. To produce this menu, PBX Inc. would have to develop new features (e.g., SMDR with account codes, preemptive fault location, and dynamic bandwidth allocation within eight hours). It was noted that these were the same features that the old guard proposed as enhancements to the current product line.

Second, significant economies of product scale would be realized because any single feature would be selected by more than 50 percent of the customers. Additional economies of scale would be achieved because the shell or hardware would be the same for all switches — the current System 30 shell. A common System 30 shell would allow PBX Inc. to introduce a new product without incurring significant retooling costs. In fact, because the current product line required three different shells, it was estimated that PBX Inc. would actually save more than $40 million in manufacturing costs.

Third, just-in-time manufacturing and inventory was estimated to save more than $25 million a year. According to majority projections, within 18 months the new product strategy would reduce operating expenses by 40 percent, increase revenues by more than 35 percent, and improve net margins by 30 percent.

Beyond the financials, the majority argued that the new product strategy would give PBX Inc. a significant and dynamic competitive advantage over time. First, the concept of a customized menu representing the target segments' product requirements would quickly put PBX Inc. ahead of the competition in meeting customers' product-related needs. Moreover, tracking changing customer requirements over time promised to keep PBX Inc. one step ahead.

Second, just-in-time manufacturing, delivery, and service would improve the quality of the products, and the reduction in cycle times would help the customers upgrade their switches without it having an impact on their own cycle times. Other product-related features such as SMDR with account codes, dynamic bandwidth allocation, preemptive fault location, and Caller ID with demographics would further address target customers' strategic, operations, and telecommunications management needs (e.g., needs for product quality, expanded markets, access to market information, and cost control).

After reviewing the financial situation of the proposed target markets in the context of the new product strategy, the group decided to defer a final commitment until after a pricing strategy had been designed that satisfied PBX Inc.'s financial objectives, as well as the financial constraints under which most target market customers appeared to be operating.

Pricing

The benchmark survey revealed that most customers within the target segments were small- to medium-sized businesses that did not have access to the cash necessary to purchase a PBX outright. Furthermore, many were heavily burdened by debt, which meant they would not be inclined to borrow money to finance the purchase of a PBX. Not surprisingly, most members of the target segments were likely to buy the low-priced products. Clearly, these conditions presented a challenge.

After some discussion, the group agreed that a pricing strategy built on low cost, high value, and flexible terms would enable the new product strategy to quickly grab share from the Japanese and local telephone company competitors. To accomplish this objective, the group proposed a two-tier pricing structure. First, all customers would pay a base fixed price for the shell and a robust standard package including all the features described earlier, except dynamic bandwidth allocation and incoming number identification with demographics. These enhanced features would be separately priced.

The second component addressed the poor cash and debt position of the target segments. Rather than require the customer to pay cash or borrow money to purchase a PBX, PBX Inc. would offer the customer the option of a lease purchase.

To test this pricing structure, as well as base price and enhanced feature price sensitivity, the group commissioned focus group research. The research concentrated on the reactions of members of the target segments who were recruited using CLASSIFY®. The research suggested that the proposed pricing structure would be favorably received by the target segments. In addition, analysis identified the appropriate price points for the base and enhanced features.

After the price points were established, the group revised their product portfolio value analysis. The results indicated that the pricing strategy would require PBX Inc. to sell larger numbers of units than PBX Inc. had traditionally sold and accept smaller margins. Nonetheless, the expected margins were significantly above recent performance and these margins were well within the target financial criteria.

Once the pricing issues were resolved, the group approved the new product strategy proposed by the majority.

Positioning

The group quickly determined that a new product strategy would require repositioning at multiple levels including a general competitive repositioning of PBX Inc., repositionings of the new product line for each target segment, as well as separate positionings for senior executive decision makers and telecommunications professionals. The group decided to tackle only the general competitive repositioning of PBX Inc., delegating the remaining repositioning tasks to marketing. The group reasoned that its use of the benchmark needs to create a repositioning would establish a model that marketing could follow.

On reviewing the competitive products and positionings as well as the benchmark share projections, the group concluded that the primary competition would come from the Japanese and a new line of local telephone company products. In all cases, the competition did not permit customers to select features according to need; instead it offered fixed product packages that in many cases possessed more features than the average target segment member needed.

In addition, the group discovered that competitive advertising and promotional themes focused on the technical advantages of their products, not the benefits to business. Apparently the competition assumed that small and midsize businesses would be more concerned about the technical features.

When the group reviewed the benchmark needs and requirements of the market in general, and of the target segments in particular, several common themes emerged. At the strategic level, most potential buyers needed to expand markets under highly price-competitive conditions. To accomplish this feat, many sought innovative technologies that would enable them to control and reduce operating expenses, as well as improve their ability to deliver quality products on time to their customers. Sensitive to operating overhead and costly downtime, most customers required reliable, self-healing, adaptable, and growable telephone switching equipment that was simple to operate and maintain and did not require an investment in technical staff. Most important, the equipment had to allow them to control and minimize communications costs.

After extensive discussion, the group decided to reposition PBX Inc. and the new product line as "Your silent business partner." Themes would focus on "Helping you manage costs," "We're always there when you need us," and "The quality and flexibility you need to grow." These themes were subsequently tested in focus groups among samples of customers representing the market at large, as well as the target segments. The results were extremely positive.

Organization

As the group formulated its strategic action plan, it became apparent that effective implementation would require significant changes in PBX Inc. operations and culture. Since some of these changes were prerequisites to a strategy rollout, the group decided to incorporate plans for these changes into the strategic action plan. The recommended actions and expected benefits are outlined briefly below.

1. Design, test, and install an automated just-in-time manufacturing and inventory system providing

    *   improved quality control
    *   reduced inventory carrying costs
    *   more rapid delivery to customer

2. Design, test, and install an automated service-order entry system that would

    *   speed final delivery to customer
    *   reduce order entry errors
    *   reduce service-order entry labor overhead and cost

3. Design, test, and install an automated customer information system equipped to

    *   provide timely market and customer information
    *   establish a single integrated information source to support product development, marketing, and sales
    *   facilitate timely cross-functional integration
    *   enable faster product-to-market cycle times
    *   reduce product, marketing, and sales failure rates
    *   reduce labor costs

4. Consolidate sales and service in order to

    *   reduce operating costs
    *   speed service response times
    *   satisfy customer needs

5. Design, test, and install a just-in-time service response system that would respond to customer service requests within four hours.

6. Design, test, and install a semiannual customer needs and requirements tracking system with the capacity to

   • identify and respond to changing needs and requirements
   • track changes in segment composition and size
   • keep ahead of the competition

7. Design, test, and install a performance-monitoring system that would

   • verify the effectiveness of strategies and tactics
   • identify and correct implementation problems
   • support planning efforts

8. Educate and train sales, marketing, and product development personnel in order to create a market-driven culture and foster cross-functional cooperation.

The completed strategic action plan was submitted to the CEO and the Board of Directors for approval. After considerable debate, the plans were approved and funds were committed to support full-scale implementation. By the third quarter of 1994, product development activities had begun.

At about the same time, the first annual tracking survey was completed. The tracking survey included CLASSIFY™ to monitor the size of the segments, as well as an updated series of requirements questions to evaluate product feature needs. Additional questions measured current market size and share and intended purchases through 1996.

The results indicated that total revenues generated by Margin Sensitives, Vendor Independents, and Stable Dependents would continue to grow at a CAGR of approximately 15 percent. However, PBX Inc.'s existing product line continued to lose ground against the Japanese, Canadians, and local telephone companies. While these results would not thrill Wall Street, those involved in strategic planning at PBX Inc. were encouraged by the product requirements analysis, which reinforced the findings from a year earlier.

From the outside looking in, PBX Inc. seemed to be a sinking ship in 1995. In each quarter, the company announced layoffs in the midst of declining revenues and profits. However, the situation was not nearly as bad as it appeared. Most of the layoffs were due to efficiencies gained through integrated automation, the consolidation of sales and service, or the inability of some workers to adjust to the new market-focused, automated environment.

In January 1996, PBX Inc. introduced its new product line — The Business Companion. At a press conference later in the month, PBX Inc. announced its revolutionary Just-in-Time Guarantee. These announcements served as a signal to the competition that PBX Inc. was ready to redefine the market.

THE RESULTS — PBX INC. REVISITED IN 1999

The year 1996 was one of refinement, as expected bugs in the new automated systems appeared and were routinely corrected. Cross-functional integration of product development, marketing, and sales did not always go as smoothly as it should have. Pockets of resistance to the new market-oriented culture remained. Sales and service did not uniformly use LINK™ or CLASSIFY™. As a consequence, gaps developed in performance-monitoring data, making it difficult at the end of the year to calibrate all the cost benefits of the new strategy and processes.

Nevertheless, the year-end financials were encouraging. The new product line was a definite hit. More than 4500 units were sold at an average of $25,000 a unit. When these revenues were added to the sales of the existing product line, PBX Inc. ended the year with more than $200 million in revenues — a high for the decade and a 49 percent increase over the previous year. Profits also improved, but at a slower rate than revenues, due to the effects of the investments in automation and labor turnovers.

Encouraging signs that the market-driven strategy was working emerged from the performance monitoring data. First, more than 80 percent of the new product sales came from customers classified in Margin Sensitive, Vendor Independent, and Stable Dependent segments. In fact, PBX Inc. actually increased its share within each of these target segments by an average of more than three points. Importantly, the average cost per sale for each member of the target segments was 42 percent less than the average cost per sale in the previous year, evidence that target marketing and sales were producing considerable cost efficiencies.

By January 1999, it was clear that PBX Inc.'s market-driven strategy was a sparkling success. PBX Inc. was now the share leader. Revenues were running close to $500 million — a 350 percent gain over 1993 revenues. Moreover, operating expenses relative to revenues had declined by more than 150 percent of 1993 figures. Importantly, performance monitoring enabled PBX Inc. to pinpoint the results of actions taken. These data were used to continuously refine the effectiveness of the market-driven system. Exhibit 58 summarizes the changes in procedures and the benefits of these changes realized by PBX Inc.

By the time the competition recognized the sweeping nature and success of PBX Inc.'s strategy, PBX Inc. had accomplished the prime indicator of a successful repositioning —

Exhibit 58
PROCESS CHANGES AND IMPACTS

PROCESS CHANGES	IMPACTS
PRODUCT DEVELOPMENT	**PRODUCT DEVELOPMENT**
• USE OF BENCHMARK AND TRACKING NEEDS DATA • CUSTOMER NEEDS FOCUS • TARGET MARKET FOCUS • USE OF FOLLOW-UP CUSTOMER RESEARCH TO VALIDATE AND REFINE PRIOR TO COMMITMENT • USE OF MARKET INFORMATION SYSTEM	• IMPROVE PRODUCT DEVELOPMENT CYCLE FROM 18-24 MONTHS TO 13-15 MONTHS • REDUCE PRODUCT FAILURE RATE BY MORE THAN 100% • LOWER PRODUCT DEVELOPMENT COSTS BY 50%
MANUFACTURING AND SUPPLY	**MANUFACTURING AND SUPPLY**
• ADOPT JUST-IN-TIME MANUFACTURING • MANUFACTURE PRODUCTS ON DAILY BASIS CUSTOMIZED TO SATISFY CUSTOMER REQUIREMENTS • REQUIRE SUPPLIERS TO COMPLY WITH JIT SCHEDULES	• INCREASE PRODUCTION BY 25% WITHOUT ADDITIONAL WORKERS • TRIM INVENTORIES BY 81% • REDUCE UNIT COMPLETION TIMES FROM 160 HOURS/UNIT TO 8 HOURS/UNIT • IMPROVE PRODUCT ACCURACY BY 65% TO 99.5%
MARKETING	**MARKETING**
• USE OF BENCHMARK AND TRACKING NEEDS DATA WITH TARGET • USE OF MARKET INFORMATION SYSTEM AND MARKET ANALYTICS • CROSS-FUNCTIONAL INTEGRATION WITH PRODUCT DEVELOPMENT, SALES/SERVICE • SYSTEMATIC TESTING PRIOR TO ROLLOUT • USE OF COMPUTER ASSISTED TELEMARKETING AND MAILING CAMPAIGNS	• SUPPLIER DELIVERY SCHEDULE REDUCED FROM 6 DAYS TO 24 HOURS • MARKET CAMPAIGN DEVELOPMENT CYCLE TIMES REDUCED BY 52% • ADVERTISING AND PROMOTION BUDGETS INCREASED BY 200% • CUSTOMER AWARENESS OF PRODUCTS AND BRAND INCREASED BY 35% • SALES INCREASE BY 125%
SALES AND SERVICE	**SALES**
• INTENSIFIED TRAINING ON CUSTOMER NEEDS AND TARGET SEGMENT REQUIREMENTS • USE OF LINK TO PREQUALIFY CUSTOMERS • USE OF CLASSIFY TO REVEAL INDIVIDUAL PROSPECT NEEDS/REQUIREMENTS • USE OF MARKET INFORMATION SYSTEM TO SUPPORT SALES CALLS AND PROPOSALS	• INCREASED PROSPECT TO # SALE HIT RATE FROM 1 IN 20 TO 1 IN 5 • INCREASED SALES BY 125% • INCREASED CUSTOMER SATISFACTION BY 35% • REDUCED SALES FORCE TURNOVER BY 80%/YR
DELIVERY AND SERVICE SUPPORT	**DELIVERY AND SERVICE**
• INSTITUTE AUTOMATED ORDER # ENTRY SYSTEM • INITIATE JUST-IN-TIME DELIVERY SYSTEM • INSTITUTE 24-HOUR, 7 DAYS A WEEK BEEPER AND DESKTOP COMPUTER ACCESS TO SERVICE WITH TECHNICAL HELPDESK • INITIATE JUST- IN-TIME GUARANTEE FOR DELIVERY AND SERVICE • CREATE ONE-STOP SALES/SERVICE WITH SINGLE DEDICATED TECHNICAL REPRESENTATIVE SERVING BOTH SALES AND SERVICE FUNCTIONS	• REDUCE AVERAGE ORDER/INSTALLATION INTERVAL FROM 65 DAYS TO 29 DAYS • REDUCE SERVICE RESPONSE TIME FROM 12 TO 4 HOURS • REDUCE REPEAT SERVICE CALLS FROM 2.5/CONTACT TO 1.2/CONTACT • REDUCE PROBLEM CORRECTION MEAN TIMES FROM 6.8 HOURS TO 3.7/HOURS • INCREASE OF 56% IN SERVICE/SALES PERSONNEL BUT REDUCE SALES PERSONNEL BY 68% • REDUCE OVERALL SERVICE/SALES COSTS BY 42%

they were first to market. In the years that followed, the competition attempted to copy the market-driven approach adopted by PBX Inc. While each was successful in reducing operating costs and improving profitability, PBX Inc. was able to sustain its revenue and share advantage because it had created a market-focused culture, perfected the ability to dynamically monitor customer needs and requirements, and could quickly convert those needs into tailored solutions and service.

CONCLUSION

As consultants, we are frequently brought into situations similar to the one in which our hypothetical company found itself in 1993. In these situations, we often wonder why the client could not see the problem developing sooner, why it waited so long to act. On further probing, we discover that the client did detect the symptoms and take action. However, the initial diagnostic was incomplete, and therefore the actions taken were ineffective.

Most of you are not now staring directly down the barrel of a gun the way PBX Inc. was. Instead you face a slower, more insidious threat. When revenues flatten or margins decline, the tendency is to make cosmetic changes such as those made by PBX Inc. (e.g., increase the sales force, cut operating costs, increase advertising, or change distribution channels) and then wait for the situation to improve. Unfortunately, the situation often does get better, only to deteriorate later.

The point is, do not wait until your business is sick or lame to embrace a market-driven approach. Act now and capture the high ground before your competition does.

While we have attempted to arm you with an adaptable, detailed framework for action, we want you to leave this book with a simple message. Listen to your customers. Remember that although your customer may appear to be a single buyer, there are in fact multiple buyers, each with an agenda of needs. Build a disciplined and cost-efficient yet simple and practical system for understanding customer needs and quickly translating these needs into tailored products and services. Track your customer needs over time and adjust your products and services accordingly. Use automation to build singular, accessible market-information systems to support cross-functionally integrated diagnostics and action. Create a just-in-time delivery system. But most of all, develop an internal culture that is focused on helping your customers succeed in their businesses. In a nutshell, these are the principles of a market-driven approach.

BIBLIOGRAPHY

Beane, T. P., and D. M. Ennis. "Market Segmentation: A Review." *European Journal of Marketing* 21, no. 5 (1987): 20–42.

Bennion, M. L., Jr. "Segmentation and Positioning in a Basic Industry." *Industrial Marketing Management* 16, no. 1 (February 1987): 9–18.

Bertrand, K. "Divide and Conquer." *Business Marketing* 74, no. 10 (October 1989): 49–50, 50–54.

Bond, B. "Telecom Marketing: Calling on Friends." *Telephone Engineering and Management*, 15 February 1987, 145.

Bonoma, T. V., and B. P. Shapiro. *Segmenting the Industrial Market.* Lexington: Lexington Books, 1983.

Bouracon, D. "A New Look at Needs-Based Segmentation." *EPRI Journal*, December 1990, 12–21.

Brown, H. E., R. Shivashankar, and R. W. Brucker. "Requirements Driven Market Segmentation." *Industrial Marketing Management* 18, no. 2 (May 1989): 105–112.

Burr, R. L. "Market Segments and Other Revelations." *Journal of Consumer Marketing* 4, no. 1 (Winter 1987): 51–59.

Choffray, J. M., and G. L. Lilien. "Differences in Perceptions and Evaluation Criteria among Groups Influencing Industrial Buying Decisions." American Marketing Association Attitude Research Conference, 1979, 197–215.

Corey, E. R. "Key Options in Market Selection and Product Planning." *Harvard Business Review* 53, no. 5 (September–October 1975): 119–128.

Cravens, D. W., and C. W. Lamb, Jr. "Services Marketing—Who's the Customer and What's the Competition? *Business* 39, no. 4 (October–December 1989): 3–10.

Bibliography

Cryer, C. R., S. Hoffman, and R. Kestenbaum. "Segmentation and Direct Marketing." *Marketing Communications* 12, no. 1 (January 1987): 34–36.

de Kluyver, C. A., and D. B. Whitlark. "Benefit Segmentation for Industrial Products." *Industrial Marketing Management* 15, no. 4 (November 1986): 273–286.

Dickson, P. R., and J. L. Ginter. "Market Segmentation, Product Differentiation, and Marketing Strategy." *Journal of Marketing* 51, no. 2 (April 1987): 1–10.

Doyle, P., and J. Saunders. "Market Segmentation and Positioning in Specialized Industrial Markets." *Journal of Marketing* 49, no. 2 (Spring 1985): 24–32.

Eisenhart, T. "Segmenting Markets by Corporate Culture." *Business Marketing* 73, no. 7 (July 1988): 50–51.

Engel, J. F., H. F. Fiorillo, and M. A. Cayley, eds. *Market Segmentation: Concepts and Applications.* New York: Holt, Rinehart & Winston, 1972.

Frank, R. E., W. F. Massy, and Y. Wind. *Market Segmentation.* Englewood Cliffs: Prentice Hall, 1972.

Greenberg, M., and S. S. McDonald. "Successful Needs/Benefits Segmentation: A User's Guide." *Journal of Consumer Marketing* 6, no. 3 (Summer 1989): 29–36.

Griffin, A., and J. R. Hauser. "The Voice of the Customer." M.I.T. Marketing Center Working Paper 91–2, Sloan School of Management, Massachusetts Institute of Technology, Cambridge, Mass., January 1991.

Grønhaug, K. "Autonomous vs. Joint Decisions in Organizational Buying." *Industrial Marketing Management* 4 (1975): 265–271.

Grover, R., and V. Srinivasan. "A Simultaneous Approach to Market Segmentation and Market Structuring." *Journal of Marketing Research* 24, no. 2 (May 1987): 139–153.

Gummesson, E. "The New Marketing—Developing Long-Term Interactive Relationships." *Long Range Planning* 20, no. 4 (1987): 10–20.

Haley, R. I. "Benefit Segmentation: A Decision-Oriented Research Tool." *Journal of Marketing* 32 (July 1968): 30–35.

Bibliography

Hlavacek, J. D., and B. C. Ames. "Segmenting Industrial and High-Tech Markets." *Journal of Business Strategy* 7, no. 2 (Fall 1986): 39–50.

Hlavacek, J. D., and N. M. Reddy. "Identifying and Qualifying Industrial Market Segments." *European Journal of Marketing* 20, no. 2 (1986): 8–21.

Johansson, J. K., and I. Nonaka. "Market Research the Japanese Way." *Harvard Business Review* 65, no. 3 (May–June 1987): 16–18, 22.

Kanter, R. M. "Championing Change: An Interview with Bell Atlantic's CEO Raymond Smith." *Harvard Business Review* 69, no. 1 (January/February 1991): 119–130.

Kinal, D. "Dip into Several Segmentation Schemes to Paint Accurate Picture of Marketplace." *Marketing News*, 14 September 1984, 32.

Kotler, P. "From Mass Marketing to Mass Customization." *Planning Review* 17, no. 5 (September–October 1989): 10–13, 47.

Ljungren, R. G. "Market Segmentation." In *Business-to-Business Direct Marketing Handbook*, American Management Association, 1989.

Lodish, L. M., and D. J. Reibstein. "New Gold Mines and Minefields in Market Research." *Harvard Business Review* 64, no. 1 (January–February 1986): 168–170, 172, 174, 176, 180, 182.

Maloch, D. T. "Inside Industrial Marketing: Market Segmentation Differs Significantly in Industrial Field." *Marketing News*, 10 December 1982, 10.

"Market Share and Profitability: Strategies for Competitive Business." *Small Business Reports* 12 (October 1987): 20–23.

Moriarty, R. T. *Industrial Buying Behavior: Concepts, Issues and Applications*. Lexington: Lexington Books, 1983.

Moriarty, R. T., and D. J. Reibstein. "Benefit Segmentation in Industrial Markets." *Journal of Business Research* 14, no. 6 (December 1986): 463–486.

Mroczkowski, T. "The New Competitive World in the Television Industry—A U.S. Manufacturer's Response." *Business Quarterly*, Winter 1984, 40–44.

National Analysts. *An Overview of EPRI's Commercial Needs-Based Market Segmentation Framework.* Palo Alto: Electric Power Research Institute, 1990.

—————. *Commercial CLASSIFY-Plus User's Manual.* Palo Alto: Electric Power Research Institute, 1991.

—————. *Residential CLASSIFY-Plus User's Manual.* Palo Alto: Electric Power Research Institute, 1991.

Office of Management and Budget. *Standard Industrial Classification Manual.* Washington, D.C.: U.S. Government Printing Office, 1987.

Olivette, M. J. "Marketing Research in the Electric Utility Industry." *Marketing News*, 2 January 1987, 13–14.

Parkinson, S. T. "Management Update Supplement." *Journal of General Management* 13, no. 2 (Winter 1987): 106–111.

—————. "Management Update Supplement." *Journal of General Management* 13, no. 3 (Spring 1988): 102–107.

Perreault, W. D., Jr., and F. A. Russ. "Physical Distribution Service in Industrial Purchase Decisions." *Journal of Marketing* 40, no. 2 (April 1976): 3–10.

Peters, M. P., and M. Venkatesan. "Exploration of Variables Inherent in Adopting an Industrial Product." *Journal of Marketing Research* 10, no. 3 (August 1973): 312–315.

Pink, A. I. H. "Strategic Leadership through Corporate Planning at ICI." *Long Range Planning* 21 (February 1988): 18–25.

[Poe, R.] "Companies to Watch." *Datamation*, 1 May 1988, 64–65.

Potter, W. J., E. Forrest, B. S. Sapolsky, and W. Ware. "Segmenting VCR Owners." *Journal of Advertising Research* 28, no. 2 (April–May 1988): 29–39.

Punj, G., and D. W. Stewart. "Cluster Analysis in Marketing Research: Review and Suggestions for Application." *Journal of Marketing Research* 20 (May 1983): 134–148.

"Reaching Targets, Communicating Value Are Challenges to Marketers." *Marketing News*, 10 December 1982, 10.

Resnik, A. J., P. B. B. Turney, and J. B. Mason. "Marketers Turn to 'Counter Segmentation.'" *Harvard Business Review* 57, no. 4 (September–October 1979): 100–106.

Bibliography

Rostky, G. "Unveiling Market Segments with Technical Focus Research." *Business Marketing* 71, no. 10 (October 1986): 66, 68.

Scotton, D. W., and R. L. Zallocco, eds. *Readings in Market Segmentation.* Chicago: American Marketing Association, 1989.

Segal, M. N. "Implications of Single vs. Multiple Buying Sources." *Industrial Marketing Management* 18, no. 3 (1989): 163–178.

Shapiro, B. P. "Industrial Market Segmentation from Theory to Practice." Harvard Business School Textual Note, ICCH #1-579-066, 1978.

Shapiro, B. P., and T. V. Bonoma. "How to Segment Industrial Markets." *Harvard Business Review* 62, no. 3 (May–June 1984): 104–110.

Shuster, L. A. "The Business of Selling to Business." *Hardware Age*, August 1988, 257–263.

Smith, W. R. "Product Differentiation and Market Segmentation as Alternative Marketing Strategies." *Journal of Marketing* 21, no. 1 (July 1956): 3–8.

_____. "Retrospective Note on Market Segmentation." *Journal of Marketing Research* 15, no. 3 (August 1978): 316.

Thomas, R. J. "Industrial Market Segmentation on Buying Center Purchase Responsibilities." *Journal of the Academy of Market Science* 17, no. 3 (Summer 1989): 243–252.

Tutton, M. "Segmenting a National Account." *Business Horizons* 30, no. 1 (January–February 1987): 61–68.

Wiersema, F. D. "Advanced Segmentation's Practical Parameters." *Direct Marketing* 49, no. 11 (March 1987): 31–37.

Wilson, D. T. "Industrial Buyers' Decision-Making Styles." *Journal of Marketing Research* 8 (November 1971): 433–436.

Wilson, R. D. "Segmentation and Communication in the Industrial Marketplace." *Journal of Business Research* 14, no. 6 (December 1986): 487–500.

Wind, Y. "Introduction to Special Section on Market Segmentation Research." *Journal of Marketing Research* 15, no. 3 (August 1978): 315–316.

_____. "Issues and Advances in Segmentation Research." *Journal of Marketing Research* 15, no. 3 (August 1978): 317–337.

Bibliography

Wind, Y., and R. Cardozo. "Industrial Market Segmentation." *Industrial Marketing Management* 3 (1971): 53–164.

Woodside, A. G., R. L. Nielsen, F. Walters, and G. D. Muller. "Preference Segmentation of Health Care Services: The Old-Fashioneds, Value Conscious, Affluents, and Professional Want-It-Alls." *Journal of Health Care Marketing* 8, no. 2 (June 1988): 14–24.

Woodside, A. G., J. N. Sheth, and P. D. Bennett, eds. *Consumer and Industrial Buying Behavior.* New York: North Holland, 1977.

INDEX

account executives, 139, 141
accounting, 148
advertising:
    channels for, 142–143, 150, 180, 214
    competitive, 245–246
    for computers, 49–50, 54–56, 150–151
    coordination of, 162, 167
    cost-effectiveness of, 214
    decision making and, 157–158
    by direct contact, 159
    effectiveness of, 169
    by mail, 159
    media for, 157–159
    in newspapers, 159
    product development and, 168, 240
    promotion and, xxvi, 141
    sales calls and, 159
    targets for, 49, 150–153, 158
    on television, 8
Alcoa, 4, 16
aluminum bearings, 4
Amdahl, 100
Apple, 144
AT&T, 1, 29, 56–57, 100
auto industry, 6, 61, 224

Bell Atlantic, 100
BellSouth, 100
Besieged segment, 72, 73, 74
billing procedures, 56–57, 65, 170, 173,
    200, 219
Bloomingdale's, xxi
Bonoma, Thomas, 40–43
businesses:
    authority consolidated in, 51
    behavior of, 23
    central control in, 44

complexity of, 47, 51, 160
descriptive information on, 62
executive level in, 49–50, 52–53, 54,
    85, 86, 90, 161
functional level in, 51, 52, 53, 54, 55,
    57–59
general operations level in, 51, 52–
    53, 55, 56–57
growth of, 183, 237–238
as integrated units, 137
leaders of, xii
market-driven, 8–9, 136, 190, 191,
    224–253
medium-to-large, 3–4, 10, 34, 43–44,
    56, 87
midsize, 90, 244, 246
needs of, 33–37, 48–49
organizational structure of, 56, 60,
    240, 246–249
planning by, 56, 65, 131–133, 174–
    175
purchasing behavior in, 48–51
small, 3, 10, 51, 90, 100, 244, 246
spheres of influence in, 49–50, 52
strategic level in, 51, 52, 55–56
    see also corporations
business telephone service, 5, 44, 100
Business Week, 49–50, 54, 150–151,
    157, 158

CAGR (compound annual growth rate),
    226–227, 248–249
capital:
    availability of, 48–49, 59, 65
    estimation of, 129
    investment of, 50, 60
    pricing and, 148

Index

Index

confidentiality of, 90
cross-tabulation in, 107, 186, 187, 191, 197
data from, 92, 93, 94–96, 97–98, 147, 169
discriminators in, 89
ethics of, 91
evaluation of, xii, xx, xxii, 70, 85–96
guidelines for, 88–91, 96–97, 135
inaccuracy in, 93, 95–96, 97
information sources for, 92–93, 104–107
interviews for, 70, 86, 88–91, 93–94, 135, 167
iterative procedure for, 88–91
management group for, 236–237
objectives of, 87–88, 92
product-based, 121, 195, 206–207
projections of, 93, 98
qualitative, xxv, 86, 87–91, 96, 97–98, 236
quality control for, 95
quantitative, xxv–xxvi, 91–96, 167
questionnaires used in, 92, 94, 96, 98, 134, 218, 233
sampling procedures in, 87, 89, 92–94, 97, 135
"straw men" for, 92, 139–140
survey, xxvi, 71, 86–87, 106, 107, 114, 123, 146, 164, 169
updates on, 105
validating of, 95, 114
weighting model for, 93
resource capability analysis, 103
Ries, Al, 150

sales:
channels for, 62, 104, 191, 216, 237
classification for, 197
customizing of, 134
data provided by, 20, 61, 114, 183, 198
decrease in, 114–117
direct, 181, 218
education and, 102
effectiveness of, 68, 82, 200
evaluation of, 133–134, 207
experience in, 217
figures for, 177

global, 80
hit rates in, xxiv, 83
infrastructure of, 220, 223
institutionalization of, 218
materials for, 141
M-CIS support for, 174, 175–177, 185
multiple entry points for, 160–162, 165, 166
needs-based, 217–220
performance and, 133–134, 221–223
personnel for, 220, 228
person-to-person, 165
prioritization in, 218–219
questions on, 133–134
segmentation-based, xxii, xxiv–xxv, xxvi, 66–67, 82, 84
service and, 102, 240, 247–248, 249
targets for, 49–50, 82, 120, 157, 162, 198–200, 220, 221–223
by telephone, 218
territories for, 220
training in, 216–217, 240, 248
volume of, 220
workshops for, 216
scale, economies of, xxiv, 68, 242–243
schools, multiple entry points in, 160
segmentation marketing:
accessibility of, 18, 22
actionability of, 17–18, 22
application of, 16–17, 39, 43–46
business vs. consumer, xi, xx–xxi, xxv, 23–24
combinations in, 15–17
as concept, xxvi, 2–3, 66–67, 84
data from, 204–206
definition of, xxv, 107
by demand classes, 6–7, 13
demographic, xx
durability of, 19–20, 22, 39, 40
evaluation of, 17–23
face validity of, 20, 21, 22
geographic, 6, 7, 10, 16
globalism of, 19, 22, 80–81
key concepts of, xvii–xviii
labels used in, 136
market-driven vs. product-driven continuum for, 15–17, 81–82

269

ABOUT THE AUTHORS

John Berrigan is the president of National Analysts, Inc., a respected strategic market research firm, for 20 years a division of Booz • Allen & Hamilton. He specializes in information systems, telecommunications, and utilities and has spent 10 years with National Analysts, much of that time as a partner in Booz • Allen & Hamilton. His PhD is in political science from Temple University.

Carl Finkbeiner is the director of methods at National Analysts, specializing in the development and implementation of models for business markets. He has spent nine years at National Analysts and six years at Procter & Gamble conducting market research in virtually every major industry. His PhD is in quantitative psychology from the University of Illinois.